The
FULL
PLATE

The

FULL
PLATE

Flavor-Filled,
EASY RECIPES for
Families with No Time
and a LOT TO DO

AYESHA CURRY

PHOTOGRAPHS BY EVA KOLENKO

VORACIOUS
LITTLE, BROWN AND COMPANY
NEW YORK BOSTON LODON

Voracious
Little, Brown and Company
Hachette Book Group
1290 Avenue of the Americas, New York, NY 10104
littlebrown.com

First Edition: September 2020

Voracious is an imprint of Little, Brown and Company, a
division of Hachette Book Group, Inc. The Voracious name
and logo are trademarks of Hachette Book Group, Inc.

The publisher is not responsible for websites (or their
content) that are not owned by the publisher.

The Hachette Speakers Bureau provides a wide range
of authors for speaking events. To find out more, go to
hachettespeakersbureau.com or call (866) 376-6591.

ISBN 978-0-316-49617-9 (standard hardcover) /
978-0-316-24200-4 (signed edition) /
978-0-316-24180-9 (Black Friday signed edition)
LCCN 2020936920

10 9 8 7 6 5 4 3 2 1

Photographs by Eva Kolenko
Designed by Laura Palese

WOR

Printed in the United States of America

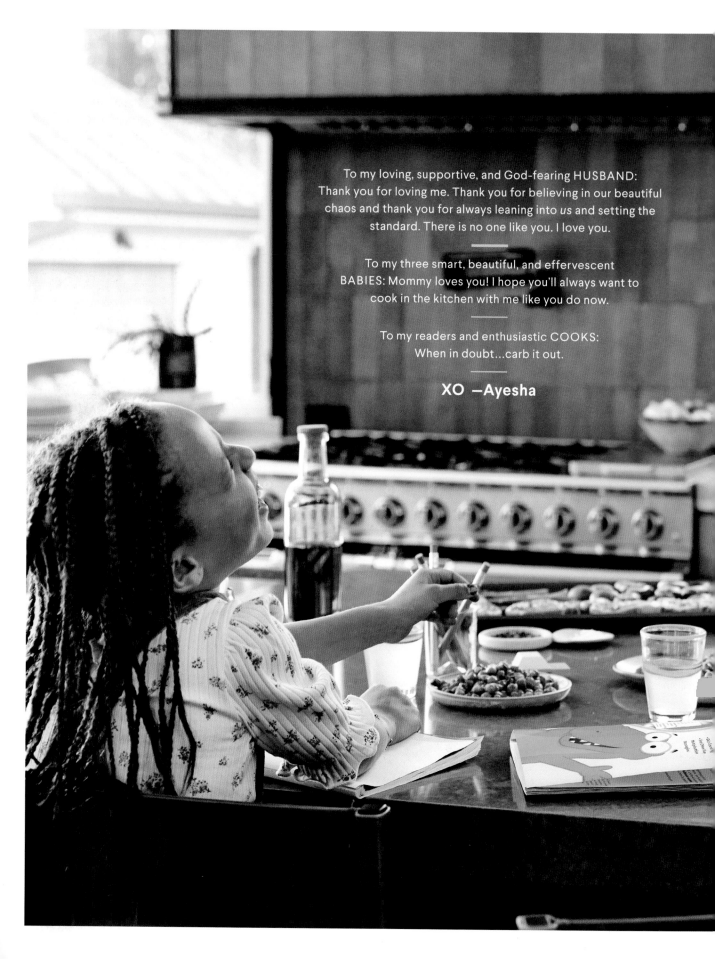

To my loving, supportive, and God-fearing HUSBAND:
Thank you for loving me. Thank you for believing in our beautiful
chaos and thank you for always leaning into *us* and setting the
standard. There is no one like you. I love you.

To my three smart, beautiful, and effervescent
BABIES: Mommy loves you! I hope you'll always want to
cook in the kitchen with me like you do now.

To my readers and enthusiastic COOKS:
When in doubt...carb it out.

XO —Ayesha

CONTENTS

INTRODUCTION

MY FULL PLATE

Food truly has enormous power. It feeds both the body and the soul. It's a vessel for communication, love, and happiness, and sets the foundation for beautiful, strong relationships of all kinds.

When I began writing my first cookbook, *The Seasoned Life,* life was so different. I was a mom of two girls, I'd truly just begun my career, and I was 26 years old. I was never sleepy, never had too much to do, and always had the flexibility to cook whatever I wanted, whenever I wanted, without time constraints.

Mealtime to us these days definitely still looks like pouring a generous glass of wine while I cook, but the logistics are *slightly* different. I mean, we blinked and suddenly there were three children! That's six legs, six arms, three heads, sixty fingers and toes (by the grace of God), *and* three very different personalities (who Stephen and I both love *equally*).

I also began my journey as an entrepreneur, started my business Sweet July, and opened three International Smoke restaurant locations in two years! Needless to say, chaos did ensue. But it's the beautiful kind of chaos that—if you replayed it in slow motion and put a string quartet behind it—could have the gravitas to coerce *all* people into having three bambinos.

In the midst of all of that, I still have this desire to nurture my family through food. That precious time together is not something I ever want to fall to the bottom of life's to-do list. But these days, I need recipes that are still full of life and flavor but take a fraction of the time to make. I've tried to give you that throughout this book. You'll notice some dishes take 10 minutes, while others take 30—and nothing is *ever* longer than an hour (major key). I want to be able to make a delicious meal for my family with enough time to actually enjoy sitting around the dinner table together.

The world was my oyster the first time around. This time, there are no pearls—or horseradish to slurp down, for that matter (ha!). Just an innate need and desire to feed my family delicious, fresh food as often as I can.

Realistically, this means focusing on dinner most days, along with a nice stiff drink for the hubs and me. I honestly don't have a ton of hacks for getting elaborate breakfasts on the table in no time. With our lives these days, that just doesn't happen—and I want to keep it real with you all. But when dinner rolls around, I can drop a few gems on how to get the meal on the table quickly while keeping it all interesting and delicious for when you do get those magical moments to gather.

My hope is that these recipes inspire you to cook with your spouse, friends, children, and loved ones more often. The kitchen is a space for infinite possibilities and a creative outlet that doesn't require too much outsourcing. I hope that through this you create gorgeous memories and moments, and that your relationships grow and grow.

Cheers to a world of possibility and a kitchen packed with flavor. We all have full plates, but these recipes will make mealtime feel worthwhile.

Let's get cooking!

—Ayesha

THE FULL PLATE PANTRY

There are some universal truths about cooking for your family: It shouldn't take a long time (none of the recipes in this book take more than an hour, and many take under 30 minutes). It shouldn't make a ton of dishes (a lot of the meals in here are of the one-pot variety). And, with the exception of a few special-occasion dishes, the recipes shouldn't require lots of expensive or hard-to-find ingredients.

A well-stocked pantry saves you time (fewer trips to the grocery store!) and makes it easier to cook a quick, delicious dinner for your family on the fly. I always keep the basics on hand, including canola and olive oils, flour and sugar, canned beans and tomatoes, dried pasta, rice, and spices—adding them to the shopping list when I've reached the last can or the bottom of the bag. If you're able, buy more than you need for a single recipe when you're out shopping. Purchase oil in big jugs and flour in 10-pound bags instead of 5 pounders (Costco is great for this). I get the 4-pound boxes of Diamond Crystal kosher salt, which is what we used when developing all these recipes. Many stores will give you a discount if you buy a whole case. If you have the storage space, buying in bulk is a great way to ensure you'll always have favorite ingredients on hand.

Beyond the basics, every chef's pantry should be tailored to what they like to cook and eat. If you like things spicy, for example, you might have a collection of hot sauces and chili pastes. If you're cooking a lot of Italian, you might stock up on tinned anchovies, tomato paste, and big hunks of Parmesan cheese (which keeps, refrigerated, for months). Here are some of the less-common ingredients I like to keep on hand to make the recipes in this book.

Spicy stuff: Many of my recipes have a little kick, so I always have a variety of spicy ingredients on hand, including sweet chili sauce (I like Mae Ploy brand), hot sauce (I like Crystal and Tapatío), chipotles in adobo sauce, and my favorite, sambal oelek, an Indonesian paste made from crushed raw chilies, vinegar, and salt.

Sweet stuff: I like to introduce a touch of sweetness to my recipes (both desserts and main courses), so I always stock honey, brown sugar (light or dark), and maple syrup, in addition to regular granulated sugar. There are a lot of crave-worthy recipes in the book that combine salty, spicy, and sweet, like the Hot Honey Chicken Sandwiches (page 48).

Dry spices: The MVPs of my dried-spice rack include curry powder (I like Betapac brand), sweet and smoked paprika, cumin (whole and ground), onion and garlic powders, and herbes de Provence.

Bottles, jars, and cans: Red wine, apple cider, balsamic, and rice wine vinegar; Dijon mustard and mayonnaise; canned tomatoes and tomato paste; canned beans; canned (or boxed) chicken stock; full-fat coconut milk; and jars of marinara (I like Rao's brand) and roasted red peppers all have permanent spots in my pantry. I often use hoisin sauce, light soy sauce, and coconut aminos (a gluten-free, slightly sweeter alternative to soy sauce, made from the aged sap of coconut blossoms), even in non-Asian recipes.

Fridge and freezer: Though the contents of my refrigerator and freezer vary from week to week, I always have the following things on hand: lemons, limes, and oranges; garlic; ginger; Parmesan cheese; frozen shrimp; and unsalted butter.

CHAPTER 1

BITES & BOOZE

SNACKS & COCKTAILS

PANCAKE-BATTERED
COCONUT SHRIMP

SERVES
4
as an appetizer
or snack

Canola oil, for frying

1 cup Krusteaz pancake mix

1½ cups sweetened shredded coconut

½ cup dark ale

1 large egg

Kosher salt

1 pound extra large shrimp (about 20), peeled and deveined with tails still intact

When Stephen and I were dating, there was nothing he loved more than a Red Baron pizza and going to the local Outback Steakhouse. I remember his order like it was yesterday: Caesar Salad, 6-ounce Victoria's Filet Mignon, Aussie Cheese Fries, and the occasional No Rules Parmesan Pasta. I, on the other hand, always opted for the Coconut Shrimp, which I have always had a soft spot for in my heart.

This is my version of that nostalgic bite. I use pancake mix for the batter, then stir in some coconut. The shrimp, dipped in the batter and fried until golden brown, are even better than the ones that inspired this recipe. If you'd like, you can make a dipping sauce by stirring together a bit of maple syrup (pancakes and syrup—get it?) and some sriracha.

Pour a 1-inch depth of canola oil into a medium heavy-bottomed pot and heat over medium-high heat until it registers 360°F on a deep-frying thermometer. Line a baking sheet with paper towels and set aside.

WHILE THE OIL HEATS, PREPARE THE BATTER SETUP: In one large bowl, put ¼ cup of the pancake mix. In another large bowl, combine the remaining ¾ cup pancake mix, ½ cup of the coconut, the ale, egg, and ½ teaspoon salt and stir until well combined. Place the remaining 1 cup coconut in a medium bowl or rimmed plate.

Pat the shrimp dry with paper towels, add to the bowl with the dry pancake mix, and toss to coat. One at a time, holding each shrimp by its tail, dip it into the batter, letting any excess drip off, then dredge in the coconut, pressing and rolling gently to coat well. Transfer to a plate.

In a few batches, fry the coated shrimp in the hot oil, turning once, until golden brown, about 2 minutes total. With a slotted spoon or spider, transfer the fried shrimp to the paper towel–lined baking sheet and season right away with a little salt. Skim the oil to remove any bits of batter, and repeat with the remaining shrimp until they have all been fried. Serve hot.

CRISPY
SWEET CHILI CHICKPEAS

1 (15-ounce) can chickpeas, drained and thoroughly rinsed

1 tablespoon extra-virgin olive oil

½ teaspoon kosher salt

2 tablespoons sweet chili sauce (such as Mae Ploy brand)

1 teaspoon grated lemon zest

1 teaspoon flaky sea salt, such as Maldon

This is the snack to make when you're short on time and ingredients but want something a little spicy, salty, and crispy. They are made with pantry staples and will satisfy any guest because they are vegan, gluten-free, and extremely crave-able.

Preheat the oven to 425°F. Spread the drained chickpeas on a clean kitchen towel in a single layer and let dry for 10 minutes (the drier the chickpeas, the crispier they'll get).

Combine the chickpeas, olive oil, and kosher salt in a bowl and toss to coat. Transfer to a rimmed baking sheet and spread in a single layer. Roast, stirring every 10 minutes, until golden brown, dry, and crispy on the outside and soft in the middle, 20 to 30 minutes.

While still hot, toss the chickpeas with the chili sauce and lemon zest and sprinkle with flaky sea salt. Serve warm.

HUSH PUPPIES

Canola oil, for frying

1 cup self-rising cornmeal

½ cup self-rising flour (see headnote)

2 tablespoons brown sugar

1 teaspoon kosher salt

1 cup buttermilk

1 large egg

½ cup crumbled cooked bacon (from about 4 slices)

2 tablespoons minced seeded jalapeño chile

2 tablespoons minced shallot

¼ cup shredded sharp cheddar cheese (optional)

Lord knows, I love a hush puppy. Though it sounds like a cute little pet, it's not. It just so happens to be the best fried food accompaniment since the almighty French fry. I hadn't tried one of these delicious morsels until I moved to North Carolina as a teenager. Give me some ribs, coleslaw, sweet tea, and some cookout hush puppies and *I'm **good** to go.*

To keep them light and fluffy, I use self-rising flour and self-rising cornmeal, and also a gentle hand when mixing in the bacon, cheese, and jalapeño. If you don't want to buy a whole bag of self-rising flour to get the ½ cup you need, make your own by combining ½ cup all-purpose flour with 1 teaspoon baking powder. And keep an eye on the oil temperature when you are frying: too cold, and the fritters will soak up oil.

You're going to love these. Eat them alone or with a yummy protein like fried chicken. *Nom nom nom.*

Heat a 2-inch depth of canola oil in a large pot or deep fryer until it registers 350°F on a deep-frying thermometer.

In a large bowl, mix the cornmeal, flour, sugar, and salt. In another bowl, whisk together the buttermilk and egg. Add the wet ingredients to the dry and stir to combine. Fold in the bacon, jalapeño, shallot, and cheddar (if using), being careful not to overmix.

Line a baking sheet with paper towels and set nearby. When the oil is hot, in batches of about 8 hush puppies, use a spoon or small scoop to scoop up batter and carefully drop into the hot oil. Fry, turning as needed and pressing each fritter into the oil to submerge it, until golden brown on all sides, 4 to 5 minutes. Use a spider or slotted spoon to remove the hush puppies from the oil and transfer to the lined baking sheet to drain. Repeat until all the batter has been used, letting the oil return to temperature between batches.

MUSHROOM TACOS
with Avocado Crema

MUSHROOMS AND MARINADE

2 tablespoons extra-virgin olive oil

1 tablespoon balsamic vinegar

1 tablespoon maple syrup

1½ teaspoons light soy sauce

Pinch red pepper flakes

6 portobello mushroom caps, sliced into ⅓-inch slices

AVOCADO CREMA

1 Hass avocado, pitted and peeled

¼ cup Greek yogurt

1 garlic clove, roughly chopped

1½ teaspoons minced, seeded jalapeño chile

Juice of ½ lime

Kosher salt and freshly ground black pepper, to taste

8 corn or flour tortillas, warmed, for serving

I developed this recipe for my sweet niece Snoh, a vegan. While the tacos aren't *completely* vegan as-is, they can be with an uber-simple swap of coconut or cashew yogurt for the Greek yogurt, and they can be gluten-free if you use tamari in place of soy, and corn tortillas instead of flour. I know Snoh will love these tacos for years to come.

Mushrooms are a great meat-free alternative when making tacos, and while I call for portobellos (for their meaty texture), you can use virtually any kind here. So whether you are vegetarian, vegan, or simply want to eat a little less meat, this recipe is for you. The crema is delicious and has a little kick from jalapeño, but that can be modified if you're not into a bit of heat.

MARINATE THE MUSHROOMS: **In a large bowl, whisk** together the olive oil, vinegar, maple syrup, soy sauce, and red pepper flakes. Add the mushroom slices and toss to coat; let sit for at least 10 minutes, or up to 30 minutes.

MAKE THE AVOCADO CREMA: **Combine all the ingredients** in the bowl of a food processor and pulse until smooth. Transfer to a bowl and season to taste with salt and pepper.

Heat a large skillet over medium-high heat. Add the mushroom slices and cook, turning as needed, until they have released their moisture and are beginning to brown and shrink, 8 to 9 minutes. Season to taste with salt and pepper.

To serve, pile some of the mushrooms onto the warmed tortillas and top with spoonfuls of avocado crema.

Note

To warm your tortillas, quickly grill over an open gas flame on its lowest setting for 30 to 40 seconds per side. Wrap in a towel to keep warm until serving.

SHRIMP
"CEVICHE"

SERVES

4

as a first course,
6 to 10 as a snack
or appetizer

Juice of 2 limes

2 tablespoons coconut
aminos (or light soy sauce)

1 tablespoon honey

Kosher salt and freshly
ground black pepper, to
taste

1 pound large (31 to 40
count) cooked shrimp

1 large mango, pitted,
peeled, and finely diced
(about 1¼ cups)

½ red onion, finely diced
(about ½ cup)

1 serrano chile, seeded and
finely diced

1 tablespoon minced fresh
cilantro

Tortilla chips or endive
leaves, for serving

This recipe was one of the first I developed for this book! I whipped it up for my first cocktail-tasting night and everyone *loved* it. Not a trace of it was left.

I'm at the point in life where at least one of my friends or family is pregnant at any given time, so it's nice to have this ceviche-like alternative to satiate their cravings, because it doesn't have raw fish! (Ceviche is typically made with raw fish that is "cooked" by the acid in citrus juice. Though the acidic marinade gives the seafood a cooked texture, it may not kill all of the bacteria. My recipe uses cooked shrimp—along with fresh mango, chile, lime, and cilantro—so it's okay for anyone to eat.)

The "ceviche" is perfect for watching games, a pre-dinner gathering, a light lunch, or in my case, an epic house party. Try it as a snack or first course with tortilla chips, spooned onto endive spears, or spooned into avocado halves.

In a small bowl, whisk together the lime juice, coconut aminos, and honey. Season to taste with salt and pepper and set aside.

Cut the shrimp into bite-size pieces and transfer to a serving bowl; add the mango, red onion, chile, and cilantro and stir to combine.

Toss the lime mixture into the bowl with the shrimp and stir until all ingredients are well coated. Season to taste with additional salt and pepper. Serve immediately, with tortilla chips or endive leaves.

SMOKED SALMON DIP

SERVES
6 to 8
as an appetizer

8 ounces cream cheese, at room temperature

½ cup plain full-fat Greek yogurt

1 tablespoon fresh lemon juice

1 small shallot, finely chopped

1 tablespoon chopped fresh dill, plus a few sprigs for garnish

1 tablespoon minced, seeded jalapeño chile

1 tablespoon capers, rinsed

½ teaspoon garlic powder

½ teaspoon smoked paprika

4 ounces smoked salmon

¼ cup minced celery

Kosher salt and freshly ground black pepper, to taste

1½ teaspoons sriracha (optional)

Pita chips, for serving

This dip gives you all the flavors of a lazy Sunday morning bagel breakfast—combined! Though the ingredient list may look long, nearly everything just gets tossed in the bowl of your food processor and whizzed together—it couldn't be simpler. Serve with pita chips, or try bagel chips or sliced vegetables (I especially like cucumbers).

In a food processor, combine the cream cheese, yogurt, lemon juice, shallot, dill, jalapeño, capers, garlic powder, and smoked paprika. Process until thoroughly combined. Add the smoked salmon and pulse until the salmon is well incorporated.

Transfer to a medium bowl and stir in the celery. Season to taste with salt, pepper, and sriracha (if using). Refrigerate for 20 minutes before serving; the dip will keep, refrigerated, for up to a week. Garnish with dill sprigs and serve with pita chips.

CHICKEN BITES

with Ooooh Mommy! Sauce

OOOOH MOMMY! SAUCE

¼ cup mayonnaise

1 tablespoon ketchup (I like Sir Kensington's or good old Heinz)

1 tablespoon honey

½ teaspoon ground turmeric

Juice of ½ lime

Kosher salt and freshly ground black pepper, to taste

CHICKEN BITES

¼ cup light soy sauce

1 large egg

1 pound boneless, skinless chicken breasts, cut into 1-inch pieces

Canola oil, for frying

½ cup all-purpose flour

¼ cup cornstarch

1 teaspoon herbes de Provence

1 teaspoon paprika

1 teaspoon kosher salt, plus additional for seasoning

Pinch of freshly ground black pepper

I created this recipe for the kiddos—but trust me when I tell you everyone will want to get their hands on these little flavor bombs. While testing this recipe with my kids, they kept asking for my "special sauce" to go along with the chicken, which was just a mix of equal parts ketchup and honey. While that combination is fine and dandy, I wanted to create a new dipping sauce for them that was truly special. Fast-forward a couple of tests and we had a sauce that had my little ones saying, "Ooooh Mommy, that's good!"

If you're gluten-free, you can go ahead and substitute gluten-free flour for the all-purpose flour in the crunchy breading; I like Bob's Red Mill brand.

MAKE THE SAUCE: In a small bowl, stir together the mayonnaise, ketchup, honey, turmeric, and lime juice. Season to taste with salt and pepper.

MAKE THE CHICKEN BITES: In a medium bowl, whisk together the soy sauce and egg. Add the chicken pieces, turn to coat, and let stand at room temperature for 10 minutes.

Meanwhile, line a rimmed baking sheet with paper towels and set nearby. Pour a 2-inch depth of canola oil into a Dutch oven or other heavy-bottomed pot and heat over high heat until it registers 375°F on a deep-frying thermometer.

In a medium bowl, combine the flour, cornstarch, herbes de Provence, paprika, salt, and pepper. Working with a few pieces of chicken at a time, remove them from the soy sauce–egg mixture, letting the excess drip off, then transfer to the bowl with the flour mixture and toss gently to coat. Transfer the breaded chicken to a clean plate; repeat until all of the chicken has been dredged in flour.

Add half the chicken to the hot oil and fry, turning once, until deep golden brown, 3 to 4 minutes. With a slotted spoon or spider, transfer to the lined baking sheet to drain. Let the oil return to temperature, then fry the remaining chicken as directed. Season the fried chicken bites with salt, transfer to a plate, and serve with the Ooooh Mommy! sauce alongside.

BRIE & PROSCIUTTO SHORTBREAD

(aka Savory S'Mores)

MAKES

8

savory
s'mores

1 (5.3-ounce) package
shortbread cookies (I like
Walkers)

4 ounces Brie cheese, cut
into 1-inch cubes

2 ounces thinly sliced
prosciutto di Parma, cut
into bite-size pieces

These indulgent little snacks can be made easily, and are a sophisticated riff on the campfire treat we all know and love. You can use round shortbread cookies or the fat fingers, then top them with Brie or another favorite soft cheese. I like to add a bit of salty prosciutto as a counterpoint to the sweet, buttery shortbread, but you could omit it if you want a vegetarian version. A bit of fruit preserves (or a small wedge of fresh pear, persimmon, fig, peach, or plum) would be a nice addition, added after the snacks come out of the oven.

Preheat the oven to 350°F. Arrange the shortbread cookies on a baking sheet in a single layer. Place a cube of Brie on top of each cookie and top with a bit of prosciutto, ruffling it slightly. Bake for 4 to 5 minutes, until the Brie has melted. Remove from the oven and let cool slightly, then serve.

CLASSIC COCKTAILS

Margarita

Makes 1 drink

2 ounces blanco tequila

1 ounce fresh lime juice

½ ounce orange liqueur, such as Cointreau

½ ounce agave syrup

Kosher salt

Lime wheel, for garnish

Combine the tequila, lime juice, liqueur, and agave in an ice-filled cocktail shaker and shake until chilled. Rim a rocks glass with kosher salt, then fill with ice. Strain the drink into the prepared glass. Garnish with a lime wheel and salt.

Manhattan

Makes 1 drink

2 ounces bourbon or rye

1 ounce sweet vermouth

2 dashes Angostura bitters

1 dash orange bitters

Brandied cherry, for garnish

Combine the bourbon, vermouth, Angostura bitters, and orange bitters in an ice-filled mixing glass and stir until well-chilled. Strain into a chilled coupe glass and garnish with a brandied cherry.

Whiskey Sour

Makes 1 drink

2 ounces bourbon

¾ ounce fresh lemon juice

½ ounce simple syrup (see page 44)

½ ounce egg white (optional)

Angostura bitters, for garnish

In an ice-filled cocktail shaker, combine the bourbon, lemon juice, simple syrup, and egg white (if using) and shake until chilled. Strain into a coupe or rocks glass and garnish with three dashes of Angostura bitters.

Sidecar

Makes 1 drink

Sugar, for rimming the glass

1½ ounces cognac

¾ ounce orange liqueur, such as Cointreau

¾ ounce fresh lemon juice

Orange twist, for garnish

Coat the rim of a coupe glass with sugar and set aside.

In an ice-filled cocktail shaker, combine the cognac, liqueur, and lemon juice and shake until chilled. Strain into the prepared glass and garnish with an orange twist.

Classic Martini

Makes 1 drink

½ ounce dry vermouth

2 ounces vodka or gin

Olive or lemon twist, for garnish

Fill a cocktail shaker with ice and add the vermouth. Stir to coat the ice, then strain the vermouth out and discard. Add the vodka to the shaker and stir well. Strain into a chilled martini glass and garnish with an olive or lemon twist.

Dirty Martini

Makes 1 drink

2½ ounces vodka or gin

½ ounce dry vermouth

½ ounce olive brine

Green olives, for garnish

Combine the vodka, vermouth, and olive brine in an ice-filled mixing glass and stir until well-chilled. Strain into a chilled cocktail glass, garnish with two olives, and serve.

Vodka Tonic

Makes 1 drink

2 ounces vodka

Tonic water, to top

Squeeze of lemon juice

Lemon peel, for garnish

In a collins glass, add the vodka and fill the glass with ice. Top with the tonic water and a squeeze of lemon juice. Garnish with a lemon peel.

MODERN COCKTAILS

Jamaican Mama

Makes 1 drink

This drink takes me back to my (now) sister-in-law Callie's bachelorette party in Jamaica. Our giant tumbler cups were filled day-round with a version of Jamaican Mama, and I wouldn't have had it any other way! It literally tastes like a tropical explosion. So, if you can't get away for vacation just yet, make this drink, take a sip, close your eyes, and *escape*.

2 ounces rum

1 ounce cognac

2 ounces fresh orange juice

1 ounce fresh lime juice

½ ounce grenadine

2 dashes aromatic bitters

Freshly grated cinnamon, for garnish

In an ice-filled cocktail shaker, combine the rum, cognac, orange juice, lime juice, grenadine, and bitters and shake until chilled. Strain into a copper mug over fresh ice. Garnish with freshly grated cinnamon.

Smoky the Bear

Makes 1 drink

This drink makes me think of big, burly men sitting around a campfire. Instead of telling scary stories, they are, for some reason, talking about their hopes and dreams, and manifesting peace and love. Now, wouldn't that be a sight?!

In all seriousness, this drink has the perfect balance of acidity, smokiness, and sweetness. It'll "put some hair on your chest" without making you cringe as though you're getting it waxed. This intro isn't getting any better…what I am saying is, make this drink if you want to feel imaginative and adventurous!

2 ounces smoky bourbon, such as Ole Smoky Straight Bourbon

1 ounce fresh lemon juice

1 ounce agave syrup

1 Amarena cherry, for garnish

Lemon twist, for garnish

In an ice-filled cocktail shaker, combine the bourbon, lemon juice, and agave and shake until chilled. Strain into a rocks glass over fresh ice. Garnish with a cherry and lemon twist.

All About That Basil

Makes 1 drink

You'll be all about the basil with no trouble when you try this smooth cocktail. (See what I did there?) I wasn't a fan of gin until recently—in my 30s. Now I love its herbaceous and floral qualities—which is why I paired it with a yummy basil-infused simple syrup. The lime rounds it out with a nice subtle pucker.

2 ounces gin

½ ounce fresh lime juice

½ ounce Basil Simple Syrup (see Note)

Fresh basil leaf, for garnish (optional)

In an ice-filled cocktail shaker, combine the gin, lime juice, and basil syrup and shake until chilled. Strain into a collins glass over fresh ice and garnish with a basil leaf, if using.

Note

TO MAKE BASIL SIMPLE SYRUP: *Combine ½ cup water and ½ cup sugar in a small saucepan over medium heat, stirring until the sugar dissolves. Let cool, then transfer to a blender. Add ½ cup fresh basil leaves and blend until smooth. Transfer to a lidded jar and refrigerate until ready to use; the syrup will keep for 1 week.*

Dirty Flower

Makes 1 drink

This drink is just so sexy! I love the bold purple hues from the crème de violette. It's perfect for a date night at home, or a ladies' night. I picture everyone in the most luxurious silk pajamas watching *The Notebook* or *The Devil Wears Prada*.

2 ounces bourbon

¼ ounce crème de violette

¾ ounce fresh lemon juice

½ ounce cherry syrup

Combine the ingredients in an ice-filled cocktail shaker and shake until chilled. Strain into a chilled coupe glass.

Peace of Pisco

Makes 1 drink

This drink says "All are welcome" from the first sip. It's fabulous as a starter drink to welcome guests before dinner, and I don't mind it as a brunch cocktail either. I typically serve it during the warmer weather months because of the brightness from the pisco and passion fruit.

3 ounces pisco

1 ounce passion fruit puree

½ ounce fresh lime juice

1 egg white

Dash of bitters

In an ice-filled cocktail shaker, combine the pisco, passion fruit puree, lime juice, and egg white and shake vigorously until the mixture is chilled and very foamy. Strain into a chilled coupe glass and garnish with a dash of bitters.

Spicy Serrano Margarita

Makes 1 drink

When I go out to eat, I order a spicy margarita so often that you could probably bet on it. I love the mix of lime, spice, and tequila. It just does something for me. We usually move into wine post-appetizer, and I find that this margarita is mild enough to not ruin the flavors of the wine. At home I love to make a big batch in a pitcher to serve to family and friends. The key to the drink not being too spicy is infusing simple syrup with chile, instead of shaking the drink with raw slices.

2 ounces tequila

½ ounce Grand Marnier

3 ounces fresh lime juice

¾ ounce Serrano Simple Syrup (see Note)

Lime wedges

Tajín seasoning, for rimming the glass

In an ice-filled cocktail shaker, combine the tequila, Grand Marnier, lime juice, and serrano syrup and shake until chilled. Rim a highball glass with a lime wedge, then dip in the Tajín. Add fresh ice to the glass, pour the drink over, and garnish with a lime wedge.

Note

TO MAKE SERRANO SIMPLE SYRUP: *Combine ½ cup water, ½ cup sugar, and 1 sliced serrano chile in a small saucepan over medium heat, stirring until the sugar dissolves. Let cool, then strain and transfer to a lidded jar. Refrigerate until ready to use; the syrup will keep for 1 week.*

So This Is Christmas

Makes 1 drink

Chestnuts roasting on an open fire...cocktails dripping out your nose. Gross? Maybe, but it fits the tune of the classic! I love this drink for any family celebration—whether it's actually Christmas or not. Perfect for cold winter months, the champagne keeps you warm and the rosemary reminds you of the crisp, fresh air.

½ ounce Rosemary Simple Syrup (see Note)

½ ounce pomegranate juice

1 teaspoon pomegranate seeds

Champagne, for topping glass

Rosemary sprig, for garnish

In a champagne flute or highball glass, combine the rosemary syrup, pomegranate juice, and pomegranate seeds. Top off the glass with champagne and add a rosemary sprig for garnish.

Note

TO MAKE ROSEMARY SIMPLE SYRUP: *Combine ½ cup water, ½ cup sugar, 1 cinnamon stick, 1 star anise, 2 cardamom pods, and 2 small fresh rosemary sprigs in a small saucepan over medium heat, stirring until the sugar dissolves. Strain, transfer to a lidded jar, and refrigerate; the syrup will keep for up to 2 weeks.*

Island Punch

Serves 8 to 10

Growing up, we had this at every family event my parents ever threw. I've elevated it a bit from its Canada Dry, canned punch, and rum days. The coconut cream makes it smooth and dreamy while the brandy and cognac make it otherwordly. This punch will definitely set the tone for your gathering, so be sure to have some great music on hand.

8 ounces Appleton Estate rum

8 ounces cognac

4 ounces pear brandy

16 ounces fresh orange juice

3 ounces fresh lime juice

4 ounces mango puree

2 ounces grenadine

2 ounces coconut cream

10 dashes bitters

Ginger ale, for serving (optional)

Fresh ginger coins, for garnish (optional)

In a large punch bowl or drink dispenser, combine all the ingredients except the ginger ale and stir until combined. To serve, fill a glass with ice and pour the punch over. If you'd like, top with a float of ginger ale.

Note

You can make it a mocktail just by leaving out the alcohol.

Blushing Rosé Sangria

Serves 6 to 8

For the ladies who brunch *or* the ladies who want to binge-watch the latest dating show on Netflix...this one is for all of you! It's so smooth, sweet, and fresh, like a gentle kiss on a summer day...*HA!* But seriously, don't plan on having one glass of this—plan on many, enjoyed in the company of your favorite friends. It's only right.

SIMPLE SYRUP

¼ cup sugar

¼ cup water

SANGRIA

1 (750ml) bottle chilled rosé wine (Whispering Angel is my jam)

8 ounces bourbon

4 ounces peach schnapps

8 ounces grapefruit juice

8 to 10 dashes grapefruit bitters

Grapefruit or peach slices, for garnish (optional)

MAKE THE SIMPLE SYRUP: In a small saucepan over medium heat, combine the sugar and water and heat, stirring, until the sugar dissolves. Remove from the heat and let cool. The syrup can be made ahead and stored in a lidded jar, refrigerated, for months.

MAKE THE SANGRIA: Pour the cooled syrup into a large pitcher and add the rosé, bourbon, schnapps, grapefruit juice, and bitters and stir well. Refrigerate for at least 1 hour before serving; the sangria will keep for 1 day.

To serve, pour into ice-filled glasses and garnish each with a grapefruit or peach slice if you like.

Ishiboo's Red Sangria

Serves 6 to 8

When I was growing up, my nickname was Ishi Bubbles, given to me because my cheeks were (and are!) so big. Now, Stephen calls me Ishiboo, and refers to this drink—which I make for party nights, taco nights, or just nights when I want to dance around the kitchen to great music—as Ishiboo's Sangria. I love that you can make it ahead so there's no stressing when you want to entertain guests.

½ cup packed brown sugar

½ cup water

1 apple, cored and sliced

1 orange, sliced and seeds removed

1 (750ml) bottle of your favorite Spanish red wine (I like a Rioja or Tempranillo)

2 ounces Grand Marnier

2 ounces apple brandy

3 ounces fresh orange juice

Orange slices, for garnish (optional)

In a saucepan over medium heat, combine the sugar, water, apple slices, and orange slices and heat, stirring, until the sugar dissolves.

Pour the syrup into a large pitcher and add the wine, Grand Marnier, apple brandy, and orange juice. Stir to mix, then refrigerate until cold. The sangria can be made up to 1 day in advance.

To serve, pour the sangria into ice-filled glasses and garnish each with half an orange slice, if you like.

CHAPTER

2

SPOONS & HANDS

SOUPS & SANDWICHES

———

HOT HONEY
CHICKEN SANDWICHES

HOT HONEY SAUCE

¼ cup honey

2 tablespoons unsalted butter

1½ tablespoons of your favorite *hot* hot sauce

CHICKEN

¾ cup all-purpose flour

¼ cup cornstarch

1 teaspoon garlic powder

2 teaspoons onion powder

2 teaspoons smoked paprika

1 tablespoon kosher salt

1 teaspoon freshly ground black pepper

1 cup buttermilk

1 teaspoon minced garlic

4 boneless, skinless chicken thighs (3 to 4 ounces each)

Canola oil, for frying

½ cup mayonnaise, optional

4 brioche hamburger buns

4 butter lettuce leaves

16 dill pickle chips

Learn to make this sandwich, and you'll never need to sit in a drive-thru ever again. It's like a Nashville hot chicken/Popeyes mash-up, but with a much more manageable level of spice and, of course, far better quality than what you'd get from a fast-food chain. The chicken is crunchy, sticky, sweet, and spicy, and you will be licking the sauce off your fingers when you're done!

MAKE THE HOT HONEY SAUCE: In a small saucepan over low heat, combine the honey, butter, and hot sauce. Heat, stirring occasionally, until the butter is melted and the sauce is smooth. Set aside.

MAKE THE CHICKEN: In a medium bowl, whisk together the flour, cornstarch, garlic powder, 1 teaspoon of the onion powder, 1 teaspoon of the paprika, the salt, and pepper. In a separate bowl, whisk together the buttermilk, garlic, remaining 1 teaspoon onion powder, and remaining 1 teaspoon paprika.

Heat a 2-inch depth of canola oil in a heavy-bottomed pot over medium-high heat until it registers 375°F on a deep-frying thermometer. While the oil heats, prepare the chicken: Dip each chicken thigh into the buttermilk mixture, letting the excess drip off. Transfer to the bowl containing the dry ingredients and turn to coat all over, then transfer to a rimmed baking sheet or plate.

Line a plate with paper towels and set nearby. Add the chicken to the hot oil and fry, turning once, until golden brown and the internal temperature registers 170°F, about 8 minutes, adjusting the heat as needed to maintain an oil temperature of about 375°F. Transfer to the paper towel–lined plate and let drain. Then transfer to a clean bowl, pour the hot honey sauce over, and toss to coat.

For each sandwich, spread both sides of the bun with mayonnaise (if using), then set one lettuce leaf on the bottom half of each bun, top with a piece of chicken and then four pickle slices. Add the top of the bun and serve immediately.

IN 'N' OUT MY KITCHEN BURGERS

SPECIAL SAUCE

¼ cup mayonnaise

1 tablespoon sweet relish

1 tablespoon ketchup

1 teaspoon brown sugar

1 teaspoon apple cider vinegar

BURGERS

1 pound ground turkey thigh

¼ cup mayonnaise

1 teaspoon onion powder

1 teaspoon garlic powder

1 teaspoon kosher salt

½ teaspoon freshly ground black pepper

1 tablespoon yellow mustard

1 tablespoon canola oil

4 slices American cheese

4 hamburger buns

Sweet onion slices (optional)

Sliced tomatoes (optional)

Shredded iceberg lettuce (optional)

It seems like no matter what day it is, the line at In 'n' Out—the beloved West Coast burger chain—is always wrapped around the building. It's been our post-game, late-night go-to for about a decade now, and the wait is always long enough to coerce me into ordering a chocolate shake.

I get it, the burger is yummy, but I wanted to do better. I wanted to create a kid-pleasing but healthy burger that I could prepare at home in the same time it would take to pull through the drive-thru. These turkey burgers with special sauce fit the bill—the addition of mayonnaise to the ground meat keeps them especially moist.

MAKE THE SAUCE: In a small bowl, stir together the mayonnaise, relish, ketchup, brown sugar, and vinegar. Set aside.

MAKE THE BURGERS: In a large bowl, combine the turkey, mayonnaise, onion powder, garlic powder, salt, and pepper and mix until incorporated. Form into four patties, each about 4 inches in diameter. Brush one side of each patty with some of the yellow mustard.

Heat the oil in a large cast-iron skillet over medium-high heat until almost smoking. Place the patties in the pan, mustard-side down, and lower the heat to medium. Cook, flipping once, until browned and cooked through, 6 to 8 minutes total; about 2 minutes before the burgers are done, top each with one slice of cheese and cover the pan so the cheese melts.

Lightly toast the hamburger buns and spread some of the sauce on both sides of the bun. Place a patty and choice of toppings on each bottom bun and top with the bun top.

CHICKEN BURGERS

with Papaya Slaw

PAPAYA SLAW

1 cup julienned fresh papaya (from 1 papaya)

½ Granny Smith apple, cored and julienned

1½ teaspoons fresh lime juice

1½ teaspoons honey

½ teaspoon red wine vinegar

Kosher salt and freshly ground black pepper, to taste

BURGERS

1 pound ground chicken thighs

1 tablespoon minced shallot

1½ teaspoons sambal oelek

1½ teaspoons minced fresh ginger

½ teaspoon kosher salt

¼ teaspoon freshly ground black pepper

2 tablespoons extra-virgin olive oil

½ cup mayonnaise

1 to 2 tablespoons sriracha

4 brioche hamburger buns, for serving

4 butter lettuce leaves

If you're looking for a lighter take on a burger, try these. I love them on a hot summer day or for a nice lunch alongside a chilled glass of rosé or hard cider. The patties are made from ground chicken seasoned with sambal and ginger, and a fresh, lime-y papaya slaw adds brightness and crunch. If you want, skip the bun and serve the patties on a bed of lettuce, with the slaw piled on top. Ground turkey is a fine substitute for the ground chicken.

MAKE THE SLAW: In a small bowl, combine the papaya, apple, lime juice, honey, and vinegar. Season to taste with salt and pepper. The slaw can be made up to a few hours ahead; refrigerate until ready to serve, draining off any accumulated juice before using.

MAKE THE BURGERS: In a medium bowl, combine the chicken, shallot, sambal, ginger, salt, and pepper and mix gently but thoroughly to combine. Form into four patties. Heat the olive oil in a large nonstick skillet over medium-high heat. When the oil is hot, add the patties and cook for 4 to 5 minutes per side, until cooked through.

In a small bowl, stir together the mayonnaise and 1 tablespoon of the sriracha; add more sriracha to taste. Spread some of the spicy mayonnaise on each side of each bun. Place a patty on the bottom half of each bun and top with some of the papaya slaw, a lettuce leaf, and the top of the bun. Serve.

CHICKEN PARM BURGERS

MAKES
4
burgers

1 pound ground chicken

3 tablespoons finely grated Parmigiano-Reggiano

2 tablespoons roughly chopped fresh basil, plus 8 leaves for serving

2 garlic cloves, minced

1 small shallot, minced

1 teaspoon Italian seasoning

1 teaspoon kosher salt

¼ teaspoon freshly ground black pepper

1 tablespoon unsalted butter

1 tablespoon extra-virgin olive oil

4 ounces fresh mozzarella cheese, cut into 8 slices

1 cup marinara sauce

4 hamburger buns

2 tablespoons mayonnaise

1 teaspoon Dijon mustard

4 romaine lettuce leaves

Everyone in my family loves chicken Parmesan, but I get bored sometimes, making it over and over and over. This is a perfect take on the traditional, *and* you don't need to bread or fry anything. So, shortcut time! I season the ground meat with basil and Parmesan cheese, form into patties, and fry up in a skillet. I then finish each burger off with a spoonful of marinara and a bit of mozzarella: A couple minutes under the broiler, and it's melty Parm perfection.

In a large bowl, combine the ground chicken, Parmigiano, chopped basil, garlic, shallot, Italian seasoning, salt, and pepper. Mix gently but thoroughly to combine, then shape into four uniform patties.

In a large skillet, heat the butter and olive oil over medium-high heat. Add the patties and cook, turning once, for 4 to 5 minutes per side, until cooked through. (You can cut into one to test, or use an instant-read thermometer: Inserted in the center of the burger, it should register 165°F.)

Preheat the broiler to low and arrange a rack 4 inches from the heating element. Transfer the cooked patties to a rimmed 11- by 13-inch baking sheet, arranging them on half of the pan. Spoon marinara sauce over the top of each patty, then top with two slices of mozzarella. Arrange the buns, cut-side up, on the other half of the pan. Broil for 2 to 3 minutes, until the cheese has melted and the buns are toasted. (Keep a close eye on the buns so they don't burn; if necessary you can pull them out before the cheese is melted.)

In a small bowl, stir together the mayonnaise and mustard and spread on each side of the toasted buns. Place a patty on each bun and top with a lettuce leaf and basil leaves and then the top of the bun. Serve immediately.

CARIBBEAN
LOBSTER ROLLS

MAKES
4
rolls

12 ounces picked fresh lobster meat (from about four 1½-pound lobsters or seven lobster tails)

½ cup mayonnaise

2 celery stalks, finely diced

1 small green apple, finely diced

¾ teaspoon curry powder (I like Betapac brand)

¼ teaspoon garlic powder

¼ teaspoon onion powder

¾ teaspoon kosher salt, plus more to taste

¼ teaspoon freshly ground black pepper, plus more to taste

1½ tablespoons unsalted butter, softened

4 hot dog buns (preferably top loaders)

I love when you can take a trip to the islands without using your passport. These rolls have that transportive quality! To give them a little island flavor, I add a hint of curry powder to the lobster; some celery and finely diced green apple provide crunch and sweetness. The lobster salad can be made ahead, but the rolls are best assembled shortly before you plan to serve them; otherwise they'll get soggy. If lobster is not available, substitute crab instead; it's just as delicious.

Chop the lobster into bite-size pieces and place in a bowl. Add the mayonnaise, celery, apple, curry powder, garlic powder, onion powder, salt, and pepper and stir to combine. Season to taste with additional salt and pepper if needed. Chill in the refrigerator for at least 15 minutes before serving. (The lobster salad can be made up to a day ahead; cover and keep refrigerated.)

Spread a thin layer of butter on each side of the hot dog buns. Place the buns buttered-side down in a large skillet and toast over medium-low heat until golden brown on one side, 2 to 3 minutes. Flip and toast on the second side. If you can't find top-loading buns, you have two options: you can simply warm the rolls (without butter), or you can trim the sides off of each bun to get a flat "butterable" surface and proceed as directed above.

Pile the lobster salad onto the toasted buns and serve right away.

STEAK SANDWICHES
with Blue Cheese & Pickled Onions

MAKES
4
sandwiches

PICKLED ONIONS

1 medium red onion, thinly sliced

1 cup warm water

½ cup white or apple cider vinegar

2 tablespoons sugar

1 teaspoon kosher salt

½ teaspoon freshly ground black pepper

STEAK

1 pound flank steak

Kosher salt and freshly ground black pepper, to taste

2 tablespoons canola oil

¼ cup mayonnaise

2 tablespoons Dijon mustard

4 ciabatta buns, split

½ cup crumbled blue cheese

1 cup loosely packed arugula

It should go without saying that this sandwich is an excellent way to use up leftover steak. I often can't finish the monster cuts of beef served at restaurants, so I'll take what's left to go and make this sandwich for lunch the next day.

If you don't have leftover steak, you can of course pan-fry (or grill!) some quick-cooking, lean flank steak for the express purpose of making these sandwiches, and you won't be sorry you did. Even though the pickled onions take a little time, I urge you to make them, because they, in turn, make the sandwich. Any leftovers can be used in a salad, like My Go-To Quinoa Salad (page 175), as a garnish for the Mushroom Tacos (page 11), or on top of a burger, like the In 'n' Out My Kitchen Burgers (page 51).

MAKE THE PICKLED ONIONS: Put the sliced onion in a bowl. In a measuring cup, combine the warm water, vinegar, sugar, salt, and pepper, then pour over the onions. Let stand at room temperature for an hour before using. The pickled red onions will keep, refrigerated, for up to 2 weeks.

COOK THE STEAK: Season the flank steak generously on both sides with salt and pepper. Heat the oil in a large cast-iron skillet over medium heat. When the oil is shimmering, add the steak and cook, turning once, until well-browned on both sides and medium rare, about 10 minutes total. Transfer to a cutting board and let rest for 5 minutes, then slice across the grain into ¼-inch-thick slices.

In a small bowl, stir together the mayonnaise and mustard. Lightly toast the buns, then spread the mayonnaise mixture on both sides of each bun. Pile some of sliced meat on the bottom half of each bun and top with some of the blue cheese, some of the pickled onions, and some of the arugula. Top with the other half of the bun. Serve.

ULTIMATE
GRILLED CHEESE

MAKES

2

sandwiches

4 slices prosciutto di Parma

2 tablespoons mayonnaise

4 slices sourdough bread

2 tablespoons apricot jam

¾ cup shredded Jarlsberg cheese

2 tablespoons unsalted butter

Savory. Sweet. Cheesy. Crispy. Goodness. I mean, what more can I say? Anyway, who doesn't love a grilled cheese sandwich? There are virtually endless possibilities when it comes to making one. As a kid, the standard was white bread slathered in butter and stuffed with American cheese before being grilled to perfection and devoured by my four siblings and me. Now my version is filled with crispy prosciutto, apricot jam, and of course, cheese—Jarlsberg in this case. I spread a little mayo on the outsides of the bread for a little extra flavor and crunch. The only thing that would possibly make this any better would probably be extra cheese?!

Preheat a large skillet over medium heat. When the pan is hot, lay the slices of prosciutto in the pan and cook, turning once, until frizzled and crisp, about 1 minute per side.

Spread the mayonnaise on one side of each slice of bread. Flip over, and spread the jam on the other sides. Divide the cheese on the jam sides of two slices of bread, top with the crispy prosciutto, and top with the remaining bread slices, jam-side down, to form two sandwiches.

Melt the butter in the skillet over medium heat. Lay the sandwiches in the pan and cook, pressing down on them occasionally with a spatula and turning once, until the bread is golden brown and the cheese is melted, about 3 minutes per side. Transfer to a cutting board and cut each sandwich in half. Serve hot.

SPICED
TOMATO & TOMATILLO SOUP

SERVES

4 to 6

2½ pounds ripe, juicy red tomatoes, cored and halved; or 2½ cups canned diced tomatoes

4 tomatillos, husks removed, halved

1 medium sweet onion, cut into wedges

1 serrano chile, stemmed and halved lengthwise

¼ cup extra-virgin olive oil

1 tablespoon garam masala

2 teaspoons kosher salt, plus more to taste

½ teaspoon freshly ground black pepper, plus more to taste

2 cups vegetable stock

2 fresh thyme sprigs

½ cup heavy cream

Sugar, if needed (see headnote)

Small basil leaves, for garnish

This soup is best when made with ripe, summer tomatoes, roasted to concentrate their natural sweetness. If you're cheating a bit and using out-of-season tomatoes, you may find that you have to add a bit of sugar to the finished soup, since the tomatillos are also acidic—even though we're only using a few of them. Or you can substitute canned, diced tomatoes (you'll need 2½ cups), in which case you don't need to roast them first. If you'd like, pluck the skins from the fresh tomatoes after they've roasted (they'll peel off easily), but if you have a good blender, this step is unnecessary. Serve bowls of this with the Ultimate Grilled Cheese (page 60).

Preheat the oven to 450°F. Spread the tomatoes, tomatillos, onion wedges, and serrano on a baking sheet and drizzle with the olive oil. Season with the garam masala, salt, and pepper and toss to coat. Roast for 30 minutes, until the skins of the tomatoes are wrinkled and the onion wedges are soft and beginning to brown.

Transfer the vegetables and any accumulated juices to the blender and blend until smooth, adding some of the vegetable stock as needed to aid the blending (you can do this in batches if necessary). Pour the pureed soup into a large saucepan and stir in the remaining stock and thyme sprigs. Bring to a boil over medium-high heat. Lower the heat to medium and simmer, stirring occasionally, for 10 minutes.

Remove and discard the thyme sprigs. Stir in the cream and season to taste with salt and pepper; if the soup tastes acidic, stir in a bit of sugar. Let simmer for 5 minutes longer, until hot. Ladle into bowls and garnish each bowl with a few small basil leaves. Serve hot.

SPOONS & HANDS: SOUPS & SANDWICHES

RED PEA SOUP

with Spinners

SERVES

4 to 6

2 tablespoons canola oil

1 large yellow onion, finely diced (about 1½ cups)

2 green onions, chopped

Kosher salt and freshly ground black pepper, to taste

2 (15.5-ounce) cans kidney beans, drained and rinsed

1 (13.5-ounce) can coconut milk

½ Scotch bonnet or habanero chile, seeded

1 large sweet potato (about 1 pound), peeled and diced

1 smoked turkey wing

4 cups chicken stock

SPINNER DUMPLINGS

1 cup all-purpose flour

¼ cup water

1 teaspoon extra-virgin olive oil

¼ teaspoon kosher salt

I was born in Canada, but I grew up knowing nothing but my Jamaican roots. My mom was born in Jamaica, as was my grandma and most of my family members. I'm a true yardie.

For my 30th birthday, Stephen surprised me with a Jamaican-themed birthday party, complete with live music from Konshens and HoodCelebrityy, the most epic video from Spice, and a three-tiered cake decorated in the country's colors: green, black, and gold. Though we didn't serve this soup at the party, we certainly could have—it's a Jamaican classic and would have fit in perfectly.

Simple and incredibly comforting, red pea soup loaded with handmade rolled-flour dumplings we call "spinners" was a staple of my childhood. On holidays growing up in Toronto we would make this on Christmas Eve, then drive around the city with a big pot in tow to feed those in need. It truly warms the soul.

In a large pot, heat the oil over medium heat. Add the yellow onion, green onions, and a generous pinch of salt and cook, stirring, until the onions are translucent, about 6 minutes. Add the beans, coconut milk, chile, sweet potato, turkey wing, and stock. Bring to a boil, then reduce the heat until the soup is simmering. Simmer for 40 minutes.

MEANWHILE, MAKE THE DUMPLINGS: In a medium bowl, stir together the flour, water, olive oil, and salt until combined. Transfer to a lightly floured work surface and knead until the dough is smooth, 2 to 3 minutes. Pinch off tablespoons of the dough and roll between your palms into fat snakes (we call these spinners).

Remove the turkey wing and chile from the soup and discard. Season the soup to taste with salt and pepper and return to a vigorous simmer. Drop the dumplings into the bubbling soup and simmer until cooked through, about 5 minutes. Ladle the soup into bowls and serve hot.

CHAPTER

3

PASTAFARIANS

NOODLES & MORE

CRAB BUCATINI

SERVES

6

1 cup cherry tomatoes

2 tablespoons extra-virgin olive oil

1 medium shallot, finely chopped

4 garlic cloves, thinly sliced

1 tablespoon tomato paste

1 (28-ounce) can crushed San Marzano tomatoes

2 tablespoons light brown sugar

2 teaspoons kosher salt

½ teaspoon ground white pepper

2 bay leaves

1 pound bucatini or spaghetti

2 cups fresh baby spinach leaves

¼ cup heavy cream

1 pound picked fresh crab meat

Handful of basil leaves, for garnish (optional)

Freshly grated Parmigiano-Reggiano, for garnish (optional)

I first had a version of this ridiculously delicious pasta in Italy, where it was served in a crab shell. We were there to celebrate my 30th birthday—10 or so of my closest ladies traveling around, eating, drinking, and experiencing new things. It was so cool! I'll never forget it. The most amazing part was that the restaurant we stopped in was not on our list of places, yet ended up being my favorite meal of the trip.

I like to use bucatini, which is a long, fat, hollow noodle, but you can substitute spaghetti if you can't find it. Crab season on the West Coast means Dungeness, and I use that sweet meat in this pasta. If there's another type of fresh crab available where you live, by all means use it! *Just not the imitation crab.* Everything else is good to go!

Bring a large pot of salted water to a boil.

Heat a high-sided skillet over medium heat. Add the cherry tomatoes to the dry pan and cook, stirring, until they begin to blister and pop, about 2 minutes. Add the olive oil, shallot, and garlic and cook, stirring, for 2 minutes more. Add the tomato paste and cook, stirring, for 1 minute, then stir in the crushed tomatoes, brown sugar, salt, white pepper, and bay leaves. Reduce the heat so the mixture is simmering and simmer for 10 minutes.

Drop the pasta into the boiling water and cook according to the package instructions. Drain, reserving 1 cup of the pasta cooking water, and return the pasta to the pot.

Stir the spinach into the sauce and cook until wilted, then pour in the cream. Add the crab meat and heat until warmed through, 2 to 4 minutes. Remove and discard the bay leaves, then pour the sauce into the pot with the pasta. Add a bit of the pasta cooking liquid and toss to coat the pasta with the sauce, adding more pasta cooking liquid as necessary so the sauce cloaks the noodles. Transfer to plates and serve warm, garnished with basil leaves and Parmigiano, if desired.

ROASTED RED PEPPER PASTA

SERVES
4 to 6

3 tablespoons extra-virgin olive oil

1 medium shallot, finely diced

1 tablespoon minced garlic

1 (16-ounce) jar roasted red peppers, drained and chopped

1 tablespoon sugar

2 teaspoons kosher salt

1 teaspoon pink peppercorns, crushed

½ cup heavy cream

1 teaspoon fresh lemon juice

1 pound dry penne rigate or rigatoni

½ cup grated Parmigiano-Reggiano

½ cup chopped fresh flat-leaf parsley

My mom isn't a lover of tomato-based sauces, so I developed this roasted pepper–based pasta for her. It's extra special because of the pink peppercorns, which have a subtle floral sweetness that I love. Store-bought roasted red peppers make the recipe a weeknight star, and their tang gives backbone to the silky sauce, which also gets an assist from a splash of heavy cream. I prefer a short pasta, like penne or rigatoni, because those shapes trap the sauce within; small shells would also be good.

Bring a large pot of salted water to a boil over high heat.

Heat the olive oil in a high-sided skillet over medium-high heat. Add the shallot and garlic and cook, stirring, for 1 minute. Add the roasted red peppers, sugar, salt, and peppercorns and cook, stirring, for 5 minutes longer. Transfer the mixture to a blender or food processor, add the cream, and blend until smooth. Return the sauce to the skillet and stir in the lemon juice.

Drop the pasta into the boiling water and cook according to the package directions until tender. Drain, reserving ½ cup of the cooking liquid.

Reheat the sauce over low heat. Add the pasta and a splash of reserved cooking water and toss so the pasta is coated in sauce. Add the Parmigiano and parsley and stir again to combine; add more of the pasta cooking water as needed so the sauce cloaks the noodles. Transfer to a serving bowl and serve immediately.

RASTA PASTA RELOADED

SERVES
8

2 pounds large (31 to 40 count) shrimp, peeled and deveined, tails removed

4 tablespoons extra-virgin olive oil

2 tablespoons light soy sauce

1 tablespoon plus 1 teaspoon jerk seasoning (I like Grace brand)

1 teaspoon sugar

½ medium red onion, diced

1 yellow bell pepper, cored, seeded, and sliced

1 green bell pepper, cored, seeded, and sliced

1 red bell pepper, cored, seeded, and sliced

2 green onions, chopped

Kosher salt and freshly ground black pepper, to taste

1 tablespoon curry powder (I like Betapac brand)

1 teaspoon ground ginger

1 teaspoon minced garlic

1 (13.5-ounce) can coconut milk

1 (14.5-ounce) can diced tomatoes

¼ cup sweet chili sauce (such as Mae Ploy brand)

1½ pounds linguini or linguini fini (thin linguini)

Juice of 1 lime

2 cups baby spinach

½ cup grated Parmigiano-Reggiano (optional)

Cilantro, for garnish (optional)

I love this recipe because it's totally fusion and extremely comforting. My Aunty Donna first made it for me, and I've since tried my best to re-create her classic. Back in Canada, *everyone* requests it from her.

So much of the food I ate growing up had elements from all over the world on one plate, and this pasta is a perfect representation of that! You've got the taste of the islands with the jerk seasoning, curry, and peppers, and you've got a heavy Asian influence from the soy and sweet chili sauces. I know you'll enjoy it because it's fast, full of flavor—and there'll be leftovers for lunch the next day (if you're lucky).

Bring a large pot of salted water to a boil over high heat.

In a medium bowl, combine the shrimp, 2 tablespoons of the olive oil, the soy sauce, 1 tablespoon of the jerk spice, and the sugar and stir to combine. Let marinate at room temperature while you make the sauce.

In a deep skillet, heat the remaining 2 tablespoons olive oil over medium-high heat. Add the onion and cook, stirring, until beginning to soften, 2 minutes. Add all the bell peppers and the green onions and a few generous pinches of salt. Cook, stirring occasionally, for about 4 minutes. Stir in the curry powder, ginger, garlic, and remaining 1 teaspoon jerk seasoning and cook, stirring, until fragrant, about 30 seconds. Add the coconut milk and tomatoes and bring to a fast simmer. Lower the heat to medium and simmer, stirring occasionally, until the peppers are tender, about 8 minutes. Remove from the heat, stir in the sweet chili sauce, and cover the pan.

Drop the linguine into the boiling water and cook according to the package instructions.

WHILE THE PASTA BOILS, COOK THE SHRIMP: Heat a large nonstick skillet over medium-high heat. When the pan is hot, add half of the marinated shrimp and cook, turning once, until browned on both sides and bright pink, 2 to 3 minutes. Transfer to a bowl and repeat with the remaining shrimp. Stir in the lime juice.

Drain the linguine, reserving 1 cup of the pasta cooking water. Add the pasta to the sauce, along with the shrimp and spinach. Toss and stir until the spinach is lightly wilted and the linguine is coated in sauce; add a bit of the pasta water if needed to thin the sauce and help it stick to the pasta. Season to taste with additional salt and pepper. Stir in the Parmigiano (if using), garnish with cilantro (if using), and serve immediately.

GNOCCHI
with Pancetta & Fig Jam

SERVES
4
as a light main
course, 6 as a
side dish

3 ounces pancetta, finely diced

1 (16-ounce) package store-bought (refrigerated) potato gnocchi

½ cup chicken stock

2 tablespoons unsalted butter

2 teaspoons fresh thyme leaves

1 tablespoon fig jam

Kosher salt and freshly ground black pepper, to taste

¼ cup grated Parmigiano-Reggiano, for serving

Okay, fantastic story here. I created this dish the night I almost lost a finger. Hear me out. It was 1 a.m., we did not have the kiddos that evening, we were hanging with a bunch of friends, and I definitely had enjoyed a couple margaritas. Someone had the bright idea (guilty) to do our own version of *Chopped* at home. These were the ingredients that I had on hand and the dish came together like magic, but…I just happened to chop the tip of my finger off in the process. My finger has since healed, but the embarrassment has not.

The moral of the story is, go ahead and make this on a weeknight (or weekend), *but* sober, completely sober.

I do love to make my own potato gnocchi when time permits, but it's usually not in the cards these days. But there's always time to dress up store-bought gnocchi. For the pancetta, which is cured but unsmoked pork, I prefer to buy it in one piece (rather than sliced), though sliced will also work. Diced bacon is a fine substitute.

Bring a large pot of salted water to a boil over high heat.

Cook the pancetta in a large skillet over medium heat, stirring occasionally, until it has rendered most of its fat and is beginning to brown, about 7 minutes. Turn off the heat.

Add the gnocchi to the boiling water and cook according to package instructions. Drain, reserving 1 cup of the cooking water.

Return the pan with the pancetta to medium heat, then add the gnocchi and stock. Cook, stirring, until the stock reduces, 3 to 5 minutes. Stir in the butter, thyme, and jam and toss to coat, adding a bit of the gnocchi's cooking liquid if needed, until the gnocchi are coated in glossy sauce. Season to taste with salt and pepper, transfer to a warmed platter, and serve with the grated Parmigiano alongside.

WILD MUSHROOM
ORZO "RISOTTO"

SERVES
4
as a main course,
6 to 8 as a
side dish

2 ounces dried porcini
mushrooms

¾ cup boiling water

2 tablespoons extra-virgin
olive oil

1 tablespoon unsalted
butter

1 shallot, minced

2 garlic cloves, minced

Kosher salt and freshly
ground black pepper, to
taste

1 cup orzo

3 cups vegetable stock

½ cup heavy cream

¾ cup grated Parmigiano-
Reggiano

Juice of 1 Meyer lemon

Chopped fresh flat-leaf
parsley, for garnish

Though risotto is typically made by stirring and stirring short-grain white rice in stock, I like to use rice-shaped orzo pasta instead of rice; the upshot is that the "risotto" comes together with much less effort. Unlike classic risotto, where you gradually add the liquid to rice and stir constantly, in this recipe all of the liquid is added at once to the orzo and you need only stir occasionally.

With Parmesan and dried mushrooms, this is an umami flavor bomb in your mouth! If you have never worked with dried mushrooms before, this is your moment. They can be slightly more expensive, but they really pack a lot of flavor. Once soaked and reconstituted, they will transform your dish. Lightly flavored with stock, Parmesan, and lemon juice, this easy orzo is the perfect side or main dish for your next meal.

Combine the dried mushrooms and boiling water in a medium bowl and let stand for 30 minutes. Remove the mushrooms from the water with a slotted spoon. Strain the soaking liquid through a fine-mesh strainer lined with paper towels or a coffee filter and reserve. Finely chop the reconstituted mushrooms and reserve.

In a large skillet with a lid, heat the olive oil and butter over medium heat until the butter melts. Add the shallot and garlic and a generous pinch of salt and cook, stirring, until fragrant, 1 to 2 minutes. Add the orzo and let toast, stirring, for 1 minute longer.

Stir in the chopped mushrooms, ½ cup of the mushroom soaking liquid, the stock, and cream. Cover, reduce the heat to medium low, and cook, stirring occasionally, for 15 to 20 minutes, until the orzo is al dente.

Stir in the Parmigiano and lemon juice and season to taste with additional salt and pepper. Stir well until the cheese melts and the risotto thickens slightly. Transfer to a bowl, garnish with parsley, and serve.

LAMB PASTA BAKE

2 tablespoons extra-virgin olive oil, plus more for greasing the baking dish

2 medium onions, diced

2 tablespoons minced garlic

2 pounds ground lamb

1 tablespoon kosher salt

1 teaspoon ground cinnamon

1 teaspoon ground nutmeg

1 teaspoon dried oregano

1 (24-ounce) jar marinara sauce

1 (8-ounce) can tomato sauce

1½ pounds short dry pasta of your choice (such as rigatoni, fusilli, or penne)

1 cup fresh basil leaves, roughly chopped

1 (15-ounce) container whole-milk ricotta

2 cups grated Parmigiano-Reggiano

This crowd-pleasing meal is hearty and incredibly satisfying, but still quick enough to be able to throw together for a weeknight dinner, and substantial enough to provide leftovers for the next day. I like to dollop on the ricotta instead of stirring it into the sauce, so the pasta is studded with depth charges of cheese. If you don't care for ground lamb, you can use ground beef or (uncased) sausage instead. Serve with a big green salad and some crusty bread.

Preheat the oven to 350°F. Bring a large pot of salted water to a boil over high heat.

In a deep skillet over medium heat, heat the olive oil. Add the onions and cook, stirring, for 2 minutes. Add the garlic and cook for 30 seconds more. Add the lamb, salt, cinnamon, nutmeg, and oregano and cook, stirring and breaking up the chunks of lamb, until the meat is no longer pink, about 7 minutes. Reduce the heat to medium, stir in the marinara sauce and tomato sauce, and mix to combine. Reduce the heat to low and let simmer, stirring occasionally, for 10 minutes.

Drop the pasta into the boiling water and cook for 2 minutes less than directed on the package. Drain, reserving 1 cup of the pasta cooking water. Return the pasta to the pot, add the meat sauce and half of the reserved pasta water, and stir to mix. Stir in the basil, and add more of the pasta cooking liquid as needed so the sauce coats the pasta.

Transfer to a greased 8- by 11-inch glass or ceramic baking dish and dollop the ricotta over the top, spacing it evenly and pressing the ricotta down slightly into the pasta. Sprinkle the Parmigiano over the top. Bake for 25 minutes, until the cheese is golden brown. Serve hot.

CRAB MAC & CHEESE

1 pound dry medium shell pasta

2 tablespoons unsalted butter

2 tablespoons all-purpose flour

2 cups half-and-half, warmed

1 cup grated Asiago cheese

1 cup grated Parmigiano-Reggiano

¼ cup sweet chili sauce (such as Mae Ploy brand)

1 teaspoon kosher salt, plus more to taste

½ teaspoon ground white pepper, plus more to taste

½ pound picked fresh crab meat

½ cup thinly sliced green onions

It's hard to improve upon macaroni and cheese, but adding crab meat is one good way to do it. This dish is so oddly satisfying, as people don't typically pair seafood and cheese, but *this works*. I like to use small shell-shaped pasta here; the folds in the noodles act as traps for the creamy sauce. Without the crab added, this is still a great version of a classic—but adding the crab makes it extra special. Lobster would be good, too.

Bring a large pot of salted water to a boil. Add the pasta and cook according to the package instructions. Drain and transfer to a large bowl.

Meanwhile, in a medium saucepan over medium heat, melt the butter. Whisk in the flour and cook, whisking, until the mixture is lightly browned and has a toasty aroma, about 2 minutes. Whisk in the half-and-half, increase the heat to medium high, and continue to cook, whisking, until the mixture bubbles and thickens. Reduce the heat to low and stir in the Asiago, Parmigiano, chili sauce, salt, and pepper and continue to cook, stirring, until smooth.

Preheat the broiler and arrange an oven rack 4 inches from the heating element. Pour the sauce over the pasta in the bowl, then stir in the crab meat and green onions. Season to taste with additional salt and pepper, then transfer to a 9-inch-square baking dish. Transfer the dish to the oven and broil until the top is golden brown, 2 to 3 minutes. Serve hot.

CHAPTER

4

UNDER THE SEA

SEAFOOD

MAHI-MAHI & PINEAPPLE
KEBABS

MAKES

8

skewers,
serving 4

⅓ cup extra-virgin olive oil

2 tablespoons fresh lime juice

1 tablespoon chipotle in adobo sauce, finely chopped

1 teaspoon whole cumin seeds

1 teaspoon kosher salt

½ teaspoon freshly ground black pepper

12 ounces mahi-mahi fillets, cut into 1-inch cubes

2½ cups 1-inch cubed fresh pineapple

1 red bell pepper, cored, seeded, and cut into 1-inch pieces

½ red onion, cut into 1-inch pieces

2 tablespoons chopped fresh cilantro leaves

Bamboo skewers, soaked in water to cover for 1 hour

When the weather finally warms up, this is the meal I want to be grilling and serving to my friends and family. If you can't find mahi-mahi, substitute another firm white fish, such as halibut. My kids get a kick out of eating the fish and pineapple cubes off the skewers, and love them with Coconut Rice (page 183) alongside.

Preheat a gas or charcoal grill for direct high-heat grilling. Whisk together the olive oil, lime juice, chipotle, cumin, salt, and pepper in a large bowl. Add the cubed fish, pineapple, bell pepper, and onion and toss to coat.

Thread alternating cubes of fish, pineapple, bell peppers, and onion onto the soaked skewers and set on a rimmed baking sheet.

Lay the kebabs on the grill grate and grill, turning once, for 4 to 5 minutes per side, until the fish is cooked through and the vegetables and pineapple develop a nice char. Transfer to a serving platter and garnish with the cilantro.

POACHED HALIBUT

with Champagne Beurre Blanc

SERVES

4

POACHED HALIBUT

2 cups fish stock

1 (13.5-ounce) can full-fat coconut milk

4 garlic cloves, peeled and crushed

Juice of 1 lime

10 black or pink peppercorns

½ teaspoon ground turmeric

2 makrut lime leaves

1 cup thinly sliced fennel

4 boneless, skinless halibut fillets (about 1½ inches thick and 4 ounces each)

Kosher salt and freshly ground black pepper, to taste

CHAMPAGNE BEURRE BLANC

½ cup dry champagne or sparkling wine

Juice of 1 blood orange (navel orange juice can be substituted)

1 cup (2 sticks) cold unsalted butter, cubed

Kosher salt and freshly ground black pepper, to taste

Fennel fronds, for garnish (optional)

The first time I served this meal to guests, I got a collective "OMG, mmmm," followed by the silence that tells you everyone's really enjoying what you've made. I knew I had to include the recipe in this book. This dish is a tad bit elevated, so I probably wouldn't make it for a weeknight meal, but I think it's nice to have some special dishes for when there's cause to celebrate. I like to serve it with the Brown Butter–Apple Sweet Potato Mash (page 179). Or, for a simpler supper, you could serve the poached fish without the beurre blanc, with rice or crusty bread alongside.

POACH THE FISH: In a high-sided skillet with a lid, combine the fish stock, coconut milk, garlic, lime juice, peppercorns, turmeric, and lime leaves. Bring to a vigorous simmer over medium-high heat, then scoop out ½ cup of the poaching liquid and set aside. Stir in the fennel.

Season the fish generously on both sides with salt and pepper. Gently slide the fish into the poaching liquid and reduce the heat so the liquid is simmering gently. Poach, carefully turning the fillets once, until the flesh is opaque and flakes easily when touched with the tip of a knife, 8 to 10 minutes. With a fish spatula, transfer the fish and some of the fennel to a warm platter and tent with foil to keep warm.

WHILE THE FISH COOKS, MAKE THE BEURRE BLANC: Combine the ½ cup reserved poaching liquid, champagne, and orange juice in a medium saucepan. Bring to a boil and boil until the liquid is reduced by half, about 5 minutes. Reduce the heat to low and whisk in the butter, one cube at a time, letting it melt before adding the next cube, until all of the butter has been incorporated and the sauce is velvety; do not let boil, or the sauce will separate. Season to taste with salt and pepper.

Spoon some of the beurre blanc over the fish and garnish with fennel slices from the poaching liquid and a few fennel fronds, if you like. Serve the remaining sauce in a gravy boat alongside.

LEMONY
GARLIC SHRIMP

1 pound extra jumbo (16 to 20 count) shrimp, peeled and deveined

1 tablespoon extra-virgin olive oil

½ teaspoon kosher salt

½ teaspoon freshly ground black pepper

1 tablespoon minced garlic

3 tablespoons unsalted butter, cut into 3 pieces

Grated zest and juice of 1 lemon

2 tablespoons minced fresh chives

We eat a lot of shrimp in my house, because they're versatile (Bubba from *Forrest Gump* knows all about it), they cook quickly, and of course they're yummy. This recipe is no exception—it comes together in a flash. The only challenging part about shrimp is buying it, as there are so many options at the fish counter. Almost all shrimp you buy in America is frozen on the boats right after being caught. So if you see raw shrimp at the store, it is most likely frozen shrimp that has been thawed in the store, meaning it is getting less fresh by the minute. So I usually make my way to the freezer section and buy the shrimp still-frozen, and do the defrosting myself at home. (It's a snap—just let it thaw overnight in the fridge. Or, for faster thawing, take the shrimp out of the package, put it in a bowl of cold water in the sink, and let a trickle of cold water run into the bowl while excess water goes down the drain. The shrimp should be ready to cook in about 15 minutes.) Scan the packages, looking for wild shrimp (best) or, if farmed, some designation that it has been sustainably raised.

If you live somewhere where you can get truly fresh, never-frozen, wild shrimp (in and around the Gulf of Mexico, and the Carolinas), by all means use that—and consider yourself lucky!

Spread the shrimp out in a single layer on a double thickness of paper towels and pat dry. Heat the olive oil in a large skillet over medium-high heat. When the oil is shimmering, add the shrimp, salt, and pepper. Cook, turning once, until the shrimp are pink, about 2 minutes, adding the garlic halfway through cooking. Add the butter pieces and stir until melted. Remove the pan from the heat and add the lemon zest and juice and stir to coat. Transfer to a serving platter and garnish with the chives. Serve right away over buttered linguine or some leafy greens and alongside crusty garlic bread.

SWEET & SPICY
SCALLOPS

1 pound large sea scallops (12 to 16), tendons removed

Kosher salt

2 tablespoons extra-virgin olive oil

3 tablespoons honey

2 tablespoons light soy sauce

1 tablespoon unseasoned rice wine vinegar

10 paper-thin slices jalapeño chile

2 tablespoons unsalted butter

½ teaspoon cornstarch

1 tablespoon grated lemon zest (reserve half a lemon to squeeze at the end)

Juice of ½ lemon

Though I love the simplicity of a butter-seared scallop served with a squeeze of lemon and nothing else, this recipe comes together almost as quickly and delivers a big punch of flavor with very little effort. Unless you are very spice adverse, don't skip the slices of jalapeño; their heat is tempered by the honey and the mild scallops. I feel like I'm doing my best Nobu impression when I make this dish. It's perfect for a sexy spicy date night in.

When buying scallops, look for ones that are firm and dry; avoid any that appear wet or soft. And they shouldn't have an odor: If they smell fishy, they're old. Additionally, ask for scallops that are "dry," not wet (which are soaked in water and preservatives). Yes, it's okay to ask at the fish counter!

Place scallops on a rimmed baking sheet lined with a double thickness of paper towels. Place a second double thickness of paper towels on top and press gently to blot liquid. Let scallops sit at room temperature for 10 minutes while the towels absorb moisture.

Season the scallops on both sides with salt. Heat the olive oil in a large skillet over medium-high heat. Add the scallops and cook, turning once, for 2 minutes on each side, until the scallops are opaque and lightly browned. Transfer to a rimmed platter and tent with foil.

Stir the honey, soy, vinegar, and jalapeño together in a small bowl. (If your honey is cold and proves difficult to mix with the other ingredients, warm it briefly in the microwave.) Add the mixture to the now-empty skillet and bring to a simmer over medium-low heat. Whisk in the butter, followed by the cornstarch, and cook, whisking, until the sauce thickens. Remove from the heat and whisk in the lemon zest and juice, then pour the sauce over the scallops. Serve immediately with a squeeze of lemon.

SEARED
SPICED SALMON

SERVES

4

1 tablespoon smoked paprika

½ teaspoon garlic powder

1 teaspoon kosher salt

½ teaspoon freshly ground black pepper

4 skin-on salmon fillets (4 to 5 ounces each), preferably wild

2 tablespoons extra-virgin olive oil

1 tablespoon unsalted butter

Flaky sea salt, such as Maldon, for serving

1 lemon, cut into wedges, for serving

This is my go-to recipe for salmon, which is a staple in our household (even my kids like it). It's a perfect simple main course, but I also will prepare salmon like this, let it cool, and use it to top a salad.

Though it's more expensive, I prefer wild salmon to farmed. Not only is it a more sustainable choice, but I think it has better flavor. And remember, frozen seafood is great—most wild salmon is frozen on the boats when it's caught, so it's preserved at its peak.

In a small bowl, combine the paprika, garlic powder, salt, and pepper. Pat the salmon dry with paper towels, then sprinkle the seasoning mixture liberally on the flesh and skin side of each fillet.

In a large cast-iron or nonstick skillet, heat the olive oil and butter over medium-high heat. When the butter melts and stops foaming, add the salmon fillets, skin-side down. Cook without disturbing until the salmon skin lifts easily from the pan, 2 to 3 minutes. Flip the salmon and cook about 2 minutes on the other side, until the flesh flakes easily when poked with the tip of a knife. Before serving, finish with flaky sea salt and a squeeze of lemon.

CITRUS-GLAZED
SALMON

¼ cup maple syrup

2 tablespoons fresh orange juice

2 tablespoons fresh lime juice

½ teaspoon minced garlic

½ teaspoon chile powder

4 skin-on salmon fillets (about 6 ounces each), preferably wild

Kosher salt and freshly ground black pepper, to taste

Lime wedges, for serving

Salmon is high in omega-3 fatty acids, which are essential for brain function. In other words, if you make this salmon for dinner tonight, chances are you will wake up smarter. Or at least you'll have enjoyed a great meal. Either way, it's worth a shot!

Preheat the oven to 400°F and line a rimmed baking sheet with foil.

In a small saucepan, whisk together the maple syrup, orange juice, lime juice, garlic, and chile powder. Bring to a boil over medium heat, then reduce the heat and simmer, stirring frequently, until the mixture is reduced by half and thick and syrupy. Set aside about half of the glaze for serving.

Place the salmon skin-side down on the prepared baking sheet. Season each fillet with salt and pepper, then brush liberally with the remaining citrus glaze. Bake for 10 to 15 minutes, until the salmon is no longer translucent and the flesh flakes easily when poked with the tip of a paring knife. Transfer to a serving platter, spoon over the reserved glaze, and serve immediately, with lime wedges alongside.

BAKED SCALLOPS
with Cherry Tomatoes & Parmesan

SERVES
4
as a main dish;
6 as a first course

½ cup grated Parmigiano-Reggiano

¼ cup dry white wine

3 tablespoons unsalted butter, melted

2 tablespoons extra-virgin olive oil

2 garlic cloves, minced

1 small shallot, minced

1 tablespoon Italian seasoning

½ teaspoon kosher salt

⅛ teaspoon freshly ground black pepper

12 medium sea scallops (about 1 pound)

1 cup cherry tomatoes

½ cup panko bread crumbs

2 tablespoons chopped fresh flat-leaf parsley, for garnish

Crusty bread, for serving

This is my kind of meal: It's impressive, but doesn't take a lot of time. You can serve it as a first course or a main, with some warm crusty bread alongside. It's a simple, flavor-packed preparation, and the herbed bread crumbs add nice texture to the scallops and tomatoes. My sister and I developed this recipe together and were shocked when we were only able to take a small bite because the family had discovered it and devoured it. We knew then it had to make it into the book!

See page 92 for tips on buying scallops.

Preheat the oven to 350°F.

In a small bowl, combine the Parmigiano, wine, melted butter, olive oil, garlic, shallot, Italian seasoning, salt, and pepper. Spoon a few tablespoons of the Parmesan mixture in a thin layer on the bottom of a medium casserole dish. Pat the scallops dry on paper towels, then arrange in the dish in a single layer. Scatter the tomatoes around the scallops. Sprinkle 3 tablespoons of the Parmesan mixture on top of the scallops and tomatoes. Add the panko to the remaining Parmesan mixture, then sprinkle over the top of the scallops.

Bake for 20 minutes, until the scallops are firm and opaque and the panko is light brown in spots. Broil on low for an additional 3 to 5 minutes, until the bread crumbs are golden brown. Garnish with chopped parsley. Serve hot, with slices of crusty bread.

HOISIN-GLAZED
SEA BASS

2 tablespoons hoisin sauce

1 tablespoon light soy sauce

1 teaspoon extra-virgin olive oil

Pinch of freshly ground black pepper

4 skin-on black sea bass fillets (1 inch thick and 5 to 6 ounces each)

I feel like I've seen a version of this dish on every romantic Asian-style restaurant menu, and I love it. But did you know you need literally just *five* ingredients to re-create it at a fraction of the price you'd pay in a restaurant? Sticky-sweet hoisin sauce, made from soybeans, is the magic ingredient, giving the bass an incredibly favorable labor-to-flavor ratio. If you can't find sea bass, try salmon, halibut, or cod. For a side dish, serve with simple steamed rice, or try the Ginger Cauliflower Rice on page 188.

Preheat the oven to 425°F. Line a rimmed baking sheet with foil and spray with vegetable oil spray or lightly brush with oil.

In a small bowl, stir together the hoisin sauce, soy sauce, olive oil, and black pepper. Pat the fish dry with paper towels and set skin-side down on the baking sheet. Pour some of the sauce over each fillet. Bake for 10 to 14 minutes, until an instant-read thermometer inserted in the center of each fillet registers 145°F. Serve immediately.

SWEET
SAMBAL COD

¼ cup honey

2 teaspoons light soy sauce

1 teaspoon rice wine vinegar

1 teaspoon sambal oelek

1 teaspoon cornstarch

2 tablespoons canola oil

4 cod fillets (5 to 6 ounces each)

Kosher salt and freshly ground black pepper, to taste

Thinly sliced green onions, for garnish (optional)

Lime wedges, for serving

Sambal oelek, an Indonesian chile paste seasoned with vinegar and salt, is a kitchen MVP. It can be used as a condiment, or blended with honey, soy sauce, and rice wine vinegar for a flavorful glaze to slather on mild cod, which benefits from the pick-me-up (halibut would work, too). A jar of sambal will keep a long time in your refrigerator, and once you have it on hand, you'll find ways to use it— it is great on chicken wings, too!

In a small saucepan, combine the honey, soy sauce, vinegar, and sambal. Cook over low heat, stirring, until the honey has melted and the mixture is fluid. Whisk in the cornstarch and keep warm over low heat.

Heat the oil in a medium skillet over medium-high heat. Season the cod fillets on both sides with salt and pepper and add to the hot pan. Cook, turning once, until the flesh is opaque and flakes easily when poked with the tip of a paring knife, about 2 minutes per side.

Drizzle the sauce over the fish, garnish with green onions, if using, and serve right away, accompanied by the lime wedges.

PAN-SEARED
RED SNAPPER
with Olive Relish

SERVES
4 to 6

OLIVE RELISH

3 jarred piquillo peppers, chopped (about ½ cup; you can substitute roasted red peppers)

¼ cup chopped kalamata olives

2 tablespoons minced fresh flat-leaf parsley leaves

½ teaspoon minced garlic

1 tablespoon lemon juice

2 tablespoons extra-virgin olive oil

Kosher salt and freshly ground black pepper, to taste

RED SNAPPER

4 skin-on red snapper fillets (4 to 6 ounces each)

Kosher salt and freshly ground black pepper, to taste

2 tablespoons extra-virgin olive oil

1 tablespoon unsalted butter

1 lemon wedge, for serving

I first tasted this olive relish at an Italian restaurant. It was super bright and fresh but had a subtle sweetness that made me want to put it on everything throughout the meal. Once I got home, I couldn't stop craving it. So I finally began testing my own version, just so I could have it on hand at all times. Briny and bright, it's the perfect pairing for a simply seared piece of snapper, though you could substitute another white fish, or scallops. Further testing revealed the relish is also excellent dabbed onto cold roast chicken, or served alongside crudités and bread, or spooned on a cracker with goat cheese. Olive you are going to love it! (See what I did there?! Gosh, I just relish these moments.)

MAKE THE OLIVE RELISH: In a medium bowl, combine the peppers, olives, parsley, garlic, and lemon juice. Stir in the olive oil and season to taste with salt and pepper. Set aside. The relish will keep, refrigerated, for up to three days.

SEAR THE SNAPPER: Pat the snapper fillets dry with paper towels and season on both sides with salt and pepper. Heat the olive oil and butter in a large nonstick skillet over medium-high heat. When the butter stops foaming, add the fish to the pan, skin-side down, and cook for 4 minutes. Carefully flip each fillet and cook on the second side until the fish is opaque and flakes easily when poked with the tip of a paring knife, 3 to 4 minutes longer.

Transfer to a serving platter and squeeze the lemon over the fish. Top each fillet with some of the olive relish and serve immediately.

CURRY
CRAB BAG

SERVES
4

¾ cup (1½ sticks) unsalted butter

1 small sweet onion, roughly chopped

4 garlic cloves, roughly chopped

2 tablespoons curry powder

½ cup full-fat coconut milk

1½ tablespoons Ayesha's Jamaican Green Seasoning (recipe follows)

1 teaspoon kosher salt

½ teaspoon freshly ground black pepper

2 pounds crab legs; or 2 whole Dungeness crabs (about 1½ pounds each), legs pulled off and bodies shelled and halved

½ pound fresh okra

2 fresh thyme sprigs

2 tablespoons chopped fresh cilantro

1 Scotch bonnet or habanero chile (optional)

Oven bag, for baking

There's something so festive and fun about a big pile of crab. That could be the funniest sentence of all time because on paper, *pile of crab* sounds like neither of those things. But if you use your big beautiful imagination, I'm sure you'll get what I'm saying! Think giant plastic bib on a burly grown man. I get a kick out of it every time.

In this preparation, the crab (and some okra) is flavored with curry powder and coconut milk, then baked in an oven bag until hot. The bags—which are typically marketed for cooking turkey—create a sealed, steamy environment, keeping the crab moist (and making kitchen cleanup a snap). Serve on a newspaper-covered table and encourage everyone to dig in with their hands—and since you've used an oven bag and no plates, all you have to do is roll up the newspaper and your table cleanup is complete.

Preheat the oven to 350°F.

Melt the butter in a large skillet over medium-high heat. Add the onion and cook, stirring, until beginning to soften, 3 to 4 minutes. Add the garlic and curry powder and cook, stirring, for 1 minute longer. Stir in the coconut milk, green seasoning, salt, and pepper and bring to a boil. Remove from the heat and let cool slightly.

Put the crab in a large oven bag and add the okra, thyme, cilantro, and chile, if using. Carefully pour in the coconut mixture, then seal tightly and gently shake to distribute the ingredients.

Place the bag on a rimmed baking sheet and bake for 30 minutes. Remove from the oven and carefully cut open the bag (watch out for the steam!). Scoop the mixture onto a rimmed serving platter, discarding the thyme sprigs and chile. Serve hot.

Ayesha's Jamaican Green Seasoning

Makes about 1 cup

Growing up, my mom, grandma, and all of the aunties used green seasoning to marinate basically all of their proteins—fish, pork, chicken, beef, goat, you name it! This flavor profile is the perfect base for them all, without being so overpowering that you can't layer in other flavors to make each dish unique. The cool thing about Jamaican green seasoning is that everyone makes it slightly differently, but this version is my go-to formula: a little tangy, a little sweet, and a bit spicy.

And yes, there are store-bought versions of green seasoning, but the homemade is sooooo much better, and not very time consuming to make. You want those fresh, bold flavors instead of preserved mild ones.

This makes a large batch, but it keeps in the refrigerator for a week, or can be frozen for longer storage.

½ cup vegetable oil

1 small yellow onion, chopped

1 cup chopped green onion, white and light green parts only

1 cup chopped fresh flat-leaf parsley

1 cup fresh basil leaves

4 garlic cloves, peeled

½ to 1 Scotch bonnet or habanero chile (depending on how much spice you like!), halved and seeded

Leaves from 3 fresh thyme stems

1 teaspoon minced fresh ginger

2 teaspoons white vinegar

1 teaspoon sugar

1 teaspoon kosher salt

Combine all ingredients in a food processor or blender and process or blend until pureed. Transfer to a lidded jar and refrigerate for up to 1 week. Or spoon into an ice cube tray and freeze until solid, then transfer the cubes to a plastic zip-top storage bag and freeze for up to 1 month.

CRAB & SHRIMP BAG

½ pound small yellow potatoes (about 6 small potatoes)

Kosher salt

1½ cups (3 sticks) unsalted butter

¼ cup Old Bay seasoning

2 tablespoons chile powder

2 tablespoons sweet paprika

2 tablespoons brown sugar

4 garlic cloves, roughly chopped

Juice of 1 lemon

2 pounds crab legs; or 2 whole Dungeness crabs (about 1½ pounds each), legs pulled off and bodies shelled and halved

1 pound large (31 to 40 count) shrimp, shell-on, deveined

1 pound smoked sausage (such as andouille), cut into 2-inch pieces

1 large sweet onion, cut into 12 wedges

2 large ears corn, shucked and cut into thirds

Oven bag, for baking

This "crab bag" borrows the flavors of a traditional crab boil, but because it's baked in an oven, it's simpler to pull off at home. And while it's simpler, it's no less festive (or, let's face it, messy) than the original. Make it in summertime, when you can eat outdoors.

Preheat the oven to 350°F.

Put the potatoes in a medium saucepan and cover with water. Generously salt the water, bring to a boil over high heat, and cook until the potatoes are just tender, about 10 minutes. Drain and set aside.

In a medium saucepan over medium heat, combine the butter, Old Bay, chile powder, paprika, brown sugar, and garlic. Cook, stirring, until the butter is melted. Remove from the heat and stir in the lemon juice.

Add the potatoes, crab, shrimp, sausage, onion wedges, and corn pieces to a large oven bag. Pour the butter mixture into the bag, then seal tightly and gently shake to distribute the ingredients. Place on a rimmed baking sheet and bake for 40 to 45 minutes. Remove from the oven and carefully cut open the bag (watch out for the steam!). Scoop the mixture onto a large rimmed serving platter or directly onto a newspaper-covered table and serve hot.

SHEET PAN SALMON
with Pesto Butter, Corn & Tomatoes

SERVES
4

4 ears corn, shucked

1 dry pint cherry tomatoes, halved

2 tablespoons extra-virgin olive oil

Kosher salt and freshly ground black pepper, to taste

2 tablespoons unsalted butter, softened

2 tablespoons store-bought basil pesto

4 skin-on salmon fillets (5 ounces each), preferably wild

Julienned basil leaves, for garnish (optional)

This dinner is a pure celebration of summer, featuring its starring players: corn, tomatoes, and basil pesto. There's a lot to love about this recipe: that it's easy to prepare but fresh and flavorful, and also that it tastes equally good warm or at room temperature. If you're trying to beat the heat by preparing dinner earlier in the day, make this in advance and serve it (and lots of rosé) for supper.

Preheat the oven to 400°F and line a sheet pan with parchment paper.

With a sharp knife, cut the kernels off each cob of corn into a medium bowl. Add the tomatoes and olive oil and season generously with salt and pepper. Toss to coat, then spread in an even layer on the baking sheet.

In a small bowl, combine the softened butter and pesto and season to taste with salt.

Place the salmon fillets skin-side down on top of the corn and tomatoes and season with salt. Spoon the butter mixture evenly on top of the fillets. Bake for 12 to 14 minutes, until the corn is tender, the tomatoes are soft, and the fish flakes easily when poked with the tip of a paring knife. Transfer the corn-and-tomato mixture to a platter and set the fish on top. Garnish with the basil, if using. Serve hot or at room temperature.

SHEET PAN TILAPIA
with Broccolini

SERVES
4

1 pound broccolini

3 tablespoons extra-virgin olive oil

1 tablespoon light soy sauce

1 tablespoon sweet chili sauce (such as Mae Ploy brand)

⅛ teaspoon freshly ground black pepper

1 teaspoon lemon pepper

½ teaspoon smoked paprika

1 teaspoon kosher salt

4 tilapia fillets (about 1 pound total)

1 lemon, cut into wedges, for serving

This sheet pan dinner comes to the rescue when I feel like I've overindulged and need to reset with a healthy but still satisfying meal. Tilapia is an affordable, widely available farmed fish with a medium-firm texture. To punch up its naturally mild flavor, I use a combination of lemon pepper, salt, and smoked paprika, then bake it with robustly flavored broccolini. Steamed rice or Coconut Rice (page 183) would be a nice accompaniment.

Preheat the oven to 400°F.

In a large bowl, combine the broccolini with 2 tablespoons of the olive oil, the soy sauce, sweet chili sauce, and black pepper. Toss until the broccolini is well coated. Spread on a rimmed baking sheet in an even layer. Bake for 10 minutes.

Meanwhile, in a small bowl, combine the lemon pepper, paprika, and salt. Place the fish on a large plate and season on both sides with the spice mixture; drizzle with the remaining 1 tablespoon olive oil.

After 10 minutes, set the fish on top of the broccolini and continue baking until the fish is cooked through (it should flake easily when poked with the tip of a paring knife) and the broccolini is tender, about 7 minutes longer. Transfer to a platter and garnish with the lemon wedges.

SHEET PAN
SHRIMP FAJITAS

SERVES
4

SHRIMP AND VEGETABLES

1 teaspoon sweet paprika

1 teaspoon cumin

1 teaspoon kosher salt, plus more to taste

¼ teaspoon freshly ground black pepper

1 green bell pepper, cored, seeded, and sliced

1 yellow bell pepper, cored, seeded, and sliced

1 small red onion, sliced

3 tablespoons extra-virgin olive oil

2 garlic cloves, minced

1½ pounds large (31 to 40 count) shrimp, peeled and deveined, tails removed

Juice of ½ lime

FAJITAS

Crumbled cotija cheese

Salsa (optional)

Chopped fresh cilantro leaves

1 lime, cut into wedges

8 (8-inch) flour tortillas, warmed

Get your margaritas ready and the music flowing when you make this meal. It is so full of flavor but such a breeze to put together—you can prep and cook it in under 20 minutes. The shrimp is simply seasoned with Mexican flavors, tossed with onion and peppers, and thrown onto a sheet pan. Serve with warm tortillas and all your favorite fajita toppings. This will be your next go-to weeknight meal. Taco Tuesday never sounded so good.

Preheat the oven to 400°F.

PREPARE THE VEGETABLES AND SHRIMP: In a small bowl, stir together the paprika, cumin, salt, and pepper. In a large bowl, combine the pepper slices, onion slices, 2 tablespoons of the olive oil, half the garlic, and half the spice mixture and toss to coat.

Spread the vegetables directly on a rimmed baking sheet (reserve the bowl) and roast for 20 minutes, until the peppers and onions are crisp-tender.

While the vegetables roast, in the bowl you used for the vegetables, combine the shrimp with the remaining spice mixture, remaining 1 tablespoon olive oil, and remaining garlic and toss to coat. Remove the pan from the oven and scatter the shrimp over the vegetables. Return the pan to the oven and continue to roast until the shrimp are bright pink and the vegetables are beginning to brown, 5 to 7 minutes longer. Transfer to a platter and squeeze the lime juice over. Season to taste with additional salt.

FOR THE FAJITAS: Serve the shrimp and vegetables with the cotija, salsa (if using), cilantro, and lime wedges, and let guests build their own fajitas with the warm tortillas.

Quick Chicken
Tagine, page 126

CHAPTER

5

RUFFLE SOME FEATHERS

CHICKEN

CHICKEN FRIED RICE

SERVES
4 to 6

3 tablespoons canola oil

½ medium yellow onion, diced

1 red bell pepper, cored, seeded, and diced

1 yellow bell pepper, cored, seeded, and diced

1 cup fresh or canned pineapple chunks, cut into ½-inch pieces

1 cup frozen green peas

3 garlic cloves, minced

1 teaspoon grated fresh ginger

2 large eggs, beaten

3 cups cooked jasmine rice (preferably day-old)

2 cups shredded cooked chicken breast (rotisserie chicken is fine)

¼ cup golden raisins

2 tablespoons light soy sauce (or coconut aminos)

2 teaspoons curry powder (I like Betapac brand)

1 teaspoon sambal oelek

1 teaspoon kosher salt

Finely sliced green onions and chopped cilantro leaves, for garnish (optional)

This recipe is so nostalgic to me. I moved to Los Angeles when I was 17, and soon found the cutest little Thai hole-in-the-wall down the street with the best pineapple fried rice I'd ever had (I love pineapple!). I would buy a large to-go container and ration it out for three days. Years later and miles from my favorite Thai spot, I finally tried my hand at making it at home. Success! I still make it for my family, but only when Stephen isn't home, because he doesn't like warm pineapple. Oh well, more for me!

Don't be dissuaded by the long ingredient list—this recipe comes together very quickly. For that reason, you should have all of your ingredients prepped and at the ready before you start cooking.

Fried rice is an excellent way to use up bits and bobs in your fridge; you should feel free to add other vegetables you have on hand (grated carrots, chopped mushrooms, spinach) or use different cooked protein in place of the chicken (leftover steak or pork would be great).

This is best made with rice that's at least one day old; it's drier and absorbs the seasonings better. If you don't have leftover rice, you can cook a batch of rice, then spread it out on a rimmed sheet pan and leave it to cool and dry for at least an hour before frying it up.

Heat 2 tablespoons of the oil in a large, deep skillet over medium-high heat. Add the onion and bell peppers and cook, stirring, until just starting to soften, 3 to 4 minutes. Add the pineapple and peas and cook until the peas have begun to thaw, 2 to 3 minutes longer. Add the garlic and ginger and cook until fragrant, 1 minute.

Push the vegetables off to one side of the pan and add the beaten eggs to the empty side. Stir the eggs with a rubber spatula until scrambled, then transfer the vegetables and eggs to a bowl.

Add the remaining 1 tablespoon oil to the pan and return to medium-high heat. Add the rice, chicken, raisins, soy sauce, curry powder, sambal, and salt and cook, stirring, until all of the ingredients are incorporated and the rice starts to brown slightly on the bottom, about 4 minutes. Return the vegetable-egg mixture to the pan and cook, stirring, until rewarmed and incorporated into the rice, about 2 minutes.

Transfer to a large platter and garnish with sliced green onions and cilantro leaves, if desired. Serve hot.

GENERAL AYESHA'S
HONEY CHICKEN

SERVES
6

GENERAL AYESHA'S SAUCE

2 tablespoons extra-virgin olive oil

1 green bell pepper, cored, seeded, and chopped into 1-inch pieces

1 red bell pepper, cored, seeded, and chopped into 1-inch pieces

1 tablespoon minced garlic

1 tablespoon minced fresh ginger

2 tablespoons tomato paste

¼ cup honey

¼ cup unseasoned rice vinegar

¼ cup coconut aminos (or light soy sauce)

2 tablespoons brown sugar

1 teaspoon sambal oelek

CHICKEN

Canola oil, for frying

¾ cup all-purpose flour

1 teaspoon kosher salt

1 teaspoon freshly ground black pepper

2 eggs

2 pounds boneless, skinless chicken breasts, cut into 1-inch cubes

Juice of ½ lime

4 thinly sliced green onions, white and light green parts only, for garnish

If you're a fan of General Tso's chicken, you'll love this homemade version. Like the Chinese-American takeout stalwart, my take has a sticky sauce flavored with garlic and ginger that is tossed with battered and fried chicken until the chicken is well coated. Some rice would make sense alongside, as well as a simple vegetable like steamed broccoli.

MAKE THE SAUCE: In a large skillet over medium-high heat, heat the olive oil. Add the peppers and cook, stirring, until just softened, about 4 minutes. Add the garlic, ginger, and tomato paste and cook, stirring, for 1 minute longer. Pour in the honey, rice vinegar, coconut aminos, brown sugar, and sambal and stir to combine. Bring to a boil, then turn off the heat.

MAKE THE CHICKEN: Heat a 2-inch depth of canola oil in a large Dutch oven or other heavy-bottomed, high-sided pot over medium-high heat until it registers 375°F on a deep-frying thermometer.

While the oil heats, in a medium bowl, whisk together the flour, salt, and black pepper. Crack the eggs into a second medium bowl and beat with a whisk. Working in batches, add some of the chicken cubes to the egg mixture, turn to coat, and let the excess drip off, then transfer to the flour mixture and toss to coat. Transfer the dredged pieces of chicken to a rimmed baking sheet. Set a wire rack over a second rimmed baking sheet and line the rack with paper towels.

When the oil reaches 375°F, in batches, cook the dredged chicken pieces until golden brown and cooked through, 3 to 5 minutes. With a slotted spoon or spider, transfer to the paper towel–lined rack. Repeat with the remaining chicken.

Reheat the sauce over medium heat until it's bubbling gently. Add the chicken to the sauce, stir to coat, then stir in the lime juice. Transfer to a platter and garnish with the green onions. Serve right away.

QUICK
CHICKEN TAGINE

SERVES

6 to 8

3 tablespoons extra-virgin olive oil

1 medium yellow onion, diced (about 1 cup)

pinch of salt

1 tablespoon minced fresh ginger

4 garlic cloves, minced

2 teaspoons ground turmeric

1 teaspoon freshly ground black pepper

½ teaspoon ground cinnamon

½ preserved lemon peel, finely chopped

8 pitted Medjool dates, chopped

½ cup brown lentils

4 cups chicken stock

2 teaspoons kosher salt

1 pinch saffron

1 cup pitted Castelvetrano olives

1 (15-ounce) can garbanzo beans, drained and rinsed

1 whole store-bought rotisserie chicken (3 to 4 pounds)

¼ cup chopped fresh flat-leaf parsley leaves

I have been obsessed with tagines for several years now. Named for the conical earthenware cooking vessel they're traditionally cooked in, most tagine recipes feature aromatics, meat, and vegetables cooked with fragrant spices. And while I love the flavor that comes from the traditional long-cooked tagines, they are most definitely time consuming and not for the sleepy or busy.

So I created this quick version that can be made in about 30 minutes using a beloved kitchen hack: shredded rotisserie chicken! I literally make this at least once a week. The shredded meat simmers briefly in a flavor-packed base that is rich with garlic and spices, sweetened with dates, and tangy from olives and preserved lemons. The addition of lentils and garbanzo beans makes this a hearty one-pot supper, though you can serve it with rice, couscous, or pita bread.

In a medium Dutch oven or heavy-bottomed pot over medium-high heat, heat the olive oil. Add the onion and a pinch of salt and cook, stirring, for 2 minutes. Add the ginger and garlic and cook 1 minute longer, then stir in the turmeric, black pepper, and cinnamon and cook another 30 seconds. Stir in the preserved lemon, dates, and lentils. Pour in the stock and add the salt and saffron. Bring to a boil, then reduce to a simmer and stir in the olives and garbanzo beans. Cover the skillet and cook, stirring occasionally, until the lentils are cooked through, about 25 minutes.

While the tagine cooks, pull the meat from the chicken, discarding the skin and bones. Shred the meat into bite-size pieces and set aside; you should have about 4½ cups chicken.

Stir in the chicken and cook until the chicken is warmed through, 5 minutes. Transfer to a serving dish and garnish with the parsley.

CHINESE FIVE-SPICE
FRIED CHICKEN

SERVES

4 to 6

CHICKEN AND BRINE

1 (12-ounce) bottle pilsner beer, such as Stella Artois (or your favorite)

4 cups cold water

½ cup kosher salt

¼ cup packed brown sugar

3 garlic cloves, peeled and crushed

4 bone-in skin-on chicken thighs (about 1½ pounds)

4 bone-in skin-on chicken drumsticks (about 1 pound)

COATING

1½ cups all-purpose flour

2 tablespoons smoked paprika

2 tablespoons garlic powder

2 tablespoons onion powder

1 tablespoon Chinese five-spice powder

1½ tablespoons kosher salt

2 teaspoons freshly ground black pepper

Canola oil, for frying

Honey, for drizzling (optional)

Lemon wedges, for squeezing (optional)

I've been making this recipe for my friends and family for years. I once made it for our family pastor and he said I cooked like a "big ole" grandma, which to me was an absolute compliment. I can only hope my kids and future grandbabies will be requesting this fried chicken from me when the hubs and I have reached legit "big ole" status.

For the juiciest fried chicken, I like to use bone-in dark meat pieces (here a combination of legs and thighs) and soak them in a beer brine for up to 4 hours (no longer, or the chicken will get too salty). Then I dredge the chicken in highly seasoned flour that contains an unexpected "secret" ingredient: Chinese five-spice powder, a fragrant blend of star anise, cloves, cinnamon, Sichuan pepper, and fennel seeds. To ensure ultra-crispy chicken, keep an eye on your oil temperature as you fry, allowing it to return to the proper temperature between batches.

BRINE THE CHICKEN: In a large resealable plastic bag, combine the beer, water, salt, brown sugar, and garlic. Add the chicken pieces, seal the bag, and refrigerate for at least 2 hours, but not more than 4. Remove the chicken pieces from the brine, rinse with cool water, and pat dry with paper towels. Discard the beer brine.

COAT AND FRY THE CHICKEN: In a large resealable plastic bag, combine the flour, smoked paprika, garlic powder, onion powder, five-spice, salt, and pepper. Seal the bag and shake to combine.

Heat a 2-inch depth of oil in a high-sided cast-iron pan, Dutch oven, or other heavy-bottomed skillet over medium-high heat until it registers 350°F on a deep-frying thermometer.

While the oil heats, working with two pieces of chicken at a time, transfer the chicken to the bag with the flour mixture. Seal the bag and shake until the chicken pieces are coated in the seasoned flour. With tongs, remove the chicken from the bag and set on a rimmed baking sheet. Repeat with the remaining chicken pieces; discard any remaining flour mixture.

Set a wire cooling rack over a second rimmed baking sheet, line the wire rack with paper towels, and set nearby. When the oil registers 350°F, add the chicken thighs, skin-side down, and fry for 7 minutes, adjusting the heat as needed so that the oil maintains a temperature between 300 and 325°F. Flip the chicken and continue frying on the second side for 7 minutes longer, until golden brown and an instant-read thermometer inserted into the meat registers 165°F. (If your chicken is browning quickly but is not cooked through, your oil is too hot; reduce the temperature.) Transfer to the paper towel–lined baking sheet to drain. Bring the oil temperature back to 350°F and repeat with the remaining chicken drumsticks.

Transfer the fried chicken to a platter, sprinkle with salt, and drizzle with honey and a squeeze of fresh lemon, if using. Serve hot or at room temperature.

PINEAPPLE CHICKEN THIGHS

with Spiced Turmeric Cauliflower

SERVES
6

PINEAPPLE CHICKEN

1 (20-ounce) can crushed pineapple, drained

½ cup honey

2 tablespoons minced fresh ginger

1 teaspoon garlic powder

Juice of 1 lime

2 teaspoons sweet paprika

1 teaspoon ground cinnamon

1 tablespoon kosher salt

1 teaspoon freshly ground black pepper

8 to 10 bone-in, skin-on chicken thighs (about 3 pounds)

2 tablespoons extra-virgin olive oil

CAULIFLOWER

1 head cauliflower (about 1½ pounds), cut into small florets

¼ cup extra-virgin olive oil

2 teaspoons apple cider vinegar

1 tablespoon Dijon mustard

1 teaspoon ground turmeric

½ teaspoon kosher salt

¼ teaspoon freshly ground black pepper

Thinly sliced green onions, white and light green parts only, for garnish (optional)

Chopped cilantro, for garnish (optional)

I love bone-in, skin-on chicken thighs because they roast in a fraction of the time it takes to cook a whole chicken and the dark meat is flavorful and juicy. The gingery pineapple mixture is a nice complement to the spiced meat; just keep an eye on it as it bakes and if it's getting too caramelized before the chicken is cooked through, you can lower the oven temperature slightly. The cauliflower roasts in the oven alongside the chicken, making this an easy, complete supper to pull off on a weeknight.

Preheat the oven to 400°F.

PREPARE THE CHICKEN: In a medium bowl, combine the pineapple, honey, ginger, garlic powder, and lime juice. Set aside. In a separate bowl, stir together the paprika, cinnamon, salt, and black pepper.

Sprinkle the salt mixture all over the chicken thighs, then set them in a 9- by 13-inch baking dish in a single layer and drizzle with the oil. Spoon the pineapple mixture around the chicken pieces. Roast for 15 minutes.

PREPARE THE CAULIFLOWER: In a large bowl, combine the cauliflower florets, olive oil, vinegar, mustard, turmeric, salt, and pepper. Spread on a rimmed baking sheet in an even layer.

After the chicken has roasted for 15 minutes, transfer the pan with the cauliflower to the oven and continue roasting, stirring the cauliflower occasionally, until the cauliflower is tender and browned in spots and the chicken skin is crispy and an instant-read thermometer inserted into the center of a thigh registers 170°F, 30 to 40 minutes. Transfer the cauliflower to a serving dish and garnish with green onions and cilantro, if using; serve the chicken directly from the baking dish.

SHEET PAN CHICKEN

with Chickpeas & Tomatoes

SERVES

4

1 dry pint cherry tomatoes

½ teaspoon ground cumin

½ teaspoon garlic powder

½ teaspoon onion powder

2 teaspoons chile powder

1½ teaspoons kosher salt

½ teaspoon freshly ground black pepper

4 boneless, skinless chicken breasts (5 to 6 ounces each)

1 (15-ounce) can chickpeas, drained and rinsed

3 tablespoons extra-virgin olive oil

This all-in-one supper combines lean chicken with spiced, hearty, protein-rich chickpeas and cherry tomatoes that burst as they bake, turning jammy and delicious. Though it's a complete meal on its own, I like to serve a cooked grain alongside to soak up the juices.

Preheat the oven to 400°F and line a rimmed baking sheet with parchment paper.

Spread the cherry tomatoes on one-third of the baking sheet. In a small bowl, stir together the cumin, garlic powder, onion powder, 1 teaspoon of the chile powder, 1 teaspoon of the salt, and ¼ teaspoon of the pepper. Sprinkle the mixture all over the chicken. Place the chicken in the middle of the sheet pan beside the tomatoes. Season the chickpeas with the remaining 1 teaspoon chile powder, ½ teaspoon salt, and ¼ teaspoon pepper. Spread the chickpeas in a single layer on the remaining third of the baking sheet.

Drizzle the tomatoes, both sides of the chicken, and the chickpeas with the oil. Bake for 20 to 25 minutes, until the tomatoes have burst and an instant-read thermometer inserted in the center of the thickest part of the chicken registers 165°F. Transfer the tomatoes and chickpeas to a platter and place the chicken breasts on top. Serve hot.

SHEET PAN
PAPRIKA CHICKEN
with Zucchini & Onions

3 medium zucchini, cut into 1-inch cubes

1 large red onion, peeled and cut into 8 wedges

2 garlic cloves, minced

4 tablespoons extra-virgin olive oil

Kosher salt and freshly ground black pepper, to taste

2 tablespoons sweet paprika

1½ teaspoons brown sugar

1 teaspoon ground coriander

½ teaspoon ground allspice

8 boneless, skinless chicken thighs (about 2 pounds)

I love boneless, skinless chicken thighs. The dark meat is more flavorful than breast meat, they cook quickly (but don't get dry), and chicken is (always) a blank canvas for spices of all kinds. For this sheet pan supper, I spice up thighs with sweet paprika, coriander, and allspice and pair them with zucchini and onions. To avoid mushy squash, choose zucchini that are medium to small (avoid the seedy, baseball bat–size ones at all cost) and roast 1-inch pieces at a high temperature so they caramelize and brown alongside the onions.

Preheat the oven to 450°F.

In a large bowl, combine the zucchini, onion, and garlic. Add 2 tablespoons of the olive oil, season with salt and pepper, and toss to coat.

In a large bowl, combine the remaining 2 tablespoons olive oil, the paprika, brown sugar, coriander, and allspice and stir to form a paste. Season each chicken thigh with salt and pepper on both sides. Add the chicken to the spice paste and rub the paste into each piece to coat on all sides.

Place the chicken on a rimmed baking sheet and nestle the zucchini and onion around the pieces. Bake for 30 to 35 minutes, until the vegetables are tender and the chicken is cooked through. Transfer to a serving platter and serve hot.

CHAPTER

6

NICE TO MEAT YOU

BEEF, LAMB & PORK

LAMB LOIN

with Cherry-Balsamic Glaze

SERVES

4

**4 boneless lamb loins
(about 6 to 8 ounces each)**

**Kosher salt and freshly
ground black pepper, to
taste**

**3 tablespoons extra-virgin
olive oil**

**½ cup cherry preserves
(I like Bonne Maman brand)**

¼ cup balsamic vinegar

1 tablespoon minced garlic

2 fresh rosemary sprigs

When I make this dish, I can't help but think of family gatherings and the holidays; the combination of lamb and a rosemary-scented cherry sauce just feels festive. And though the finished dish feels elegant and celebratory, it also comes together quickly, so you have more time to hang with your family and friends. If you can't find lamb loin, the glaze is also great on pork loin and pork or lamb chops.

Serve with a glass of your favorite bold red wine. My sister-in-law and I own a wine brand out of Napa called Domaine Curry Femme 31. Our Cabernet Sauvignon's cherry and plum notes along with subtle thyme truly make it a great pairing with the lamb here. If you can't get your hands on our Napa fave, a nice French red cru or Italian Amarone would also pair well.

Preheat the oven to 325°F. Line a baking sheet with foil. Season the loins all over with salt and pepper.

Heat the oil in a cast-iron skillet or other heavy-bottomed skillet over medium-high heat. When the oil is hot, add the lamb loins and sear, turning once with tongs, until brown on both sides, about 2 minutes (because lamb loins are so small, there is no need to sear them on the sides). Transfer to the prepared baking sheet.

Add the cherry preserves, vinegar, garlic, and rosemary sprigs to the oil left in the pan. Bring to a boil and boil until slightly reduced, about 2 minutes. Pour half of the glaze over the loins. Transfer the pan to the oven and roast until an instant-read thermometer inserted in the thickest part of a loin registers 125 to 130°F for medium rare, 15 to 20 minutes, or 130 to 135°F for medium, 20 to 25 minutes. Transfer the lamb to a cutting board and let rest for 10 minutes. Slice into ½-inch-thick slices and serve with the remaining glaze spooned over.

BLACK PEPPER
STEAK

3 to 4 tablespoons canola oil

2 pounds tender steak, such as boneless rib eye, cut into 2-inch pieces

½ yellow onion, chopped

8 ounces button or cremini mushrooms, chopped

½ cup coconut aminos (or light soy sauce)

2 tablespoons light brown sugar

2 tablespoons minced fresh ginger

1 tablespoon minced garlic

1 tablespoon coarsely ground black pepper

1 teaspoon cornstarch

Sliced green onions, for garnish

Steamed rice, for serving

This recipe is my take on one of my favorite Chinese take-out dishes. Often it's made using lesser cuts of beef, sliced into thin strips that are quickly stir-fried so they don't toughen, with a sauce that can be a bit on the gloopy side (though I've got to admit, I still love it!). But at home, I splurge and use large cubes of boneless rib eye, and punch up the sauce with lots of fresh ginger, garlic, and freshly ground black pepper, which gives it a little heat. Cutting the meat into bigger pieces allows you to get a nice sear without overcooking, and the rib eye cut is incredibly tender. A tablespoon of black pepper may seem like a lot, but it gives the dish a bit of heat that balances its sweetness.

Heat 3 tablespoons of the oil in a large, heavy-bottomed skillet over medium-high heat. Add the steak and cook, turning once, until browned on two sides, about 1½ minutes per side. With tongs, transfer the browned meat to a plate. If the pan is dry, add the remaining tablespoon oil. Add the onions and mushrooms to the pan and cook, stirring, until the onions are translucent and the mushrooms have given off their liquid and are beginning to brown, about 5 minutes.

While the onions and mushrooms cook, in a medium bowl, whisk together the coconut aminos, brown sugar, ginger, garlic, pepper, and cornstarch. Add the meat and its juices back to the pan with the mushrooms and onions and pour in the sauce. Bring to a boil and boil until the sauce thickens, about 1 minute. Transfer to a serving platter and garnish with sliced green onions. Serve hot, with rice alongside.

PRESSURE-COOKER
PULLED PORK TACOS

MAKES
8 to 10
servings

4 pounds boneless pork butt, cut into 4 equal pieces

1½ tablespoons kosher salt, plus more to taste

1½ teaspoons freshly ground black pepper, plus more to taste

1 small white onion, thinly sliced

6 garlic cloves, peeled

1 cup beef stock

½ cup tequila

½ cup apple cider vinegar

2 fresh thyme sprigs

TACOS

Cilantro, red onion, crema, sliced radishes, fresh sweet corn, or other flavorful toppings of your choice

Tortillas (flour or corn? It doesn't matter—you choose; just serve them warm)

The electric pressure cooker (i.e., Instant Pot) has really changed my life. Some of my favorite childhood dishes that take hours to cook can now be made in as little as an hour. My mom gets weekly requests to make oxtail from family and friends after we found this out. Using the pressure cooker in this recipe makes pulled pork so tender. You get bold flavorings from tequila, stock, vinegar, and more. Of course, you can use the shredded meat for sandwiches and quesadillas, but I reserve it for one of my faves—TACOS!

Season the pork pieces all over with the salt and pepper (this can be done up to a day in advance).

Combine half the onion and half the garlic in the bottom of an Instant Pot or other electric pressure cooker. Place the pork on top. Add the stock, tequila, and vinegar and drop in the thyme sprigs. Spread the remaining sliced onion and garlic over the top of the meat. Lock the lid on the pressure cooker, then cook on the high-pressure setting for 45 minutes. Let it come down to normal pressure and release the steam.

Remove the meat from the pot and shred using two forks. Season to taste with additional salt and pepper.

Serve the pulled pork with the taco fixin's and your favorite style of tortilla. I love to enjoy this with an ice-cold lager-style Mexican beer.

SWEDISH MEATBALLS
with Blackberry Jam

SERVES
4

BLACKBERRY JAM

2 cups blackberries

¼ cup packed dark brown sugar

1½ tablespoons fresh Meyer lemon juice

1 teaspoon vanilla extract, homemade (page 220) or store-bought

¼ teaspoon kosher salt

MEATBALLS

½ pound ground pork

½ pound ground beef

½ cup panko bread crumbs

¼ cup finely chopped shallots

2 garlic cloves, minced

1 large egg

1 teaspoon kosher salt

¼ teaspoon freshly ground black pepper

1 tablespoon olive oil

Have you ever found yourself at Ikea, hours past the time you thought you'd leave, your eyes glazed over and your stomach rumbling? Chances are good the cafeteria seemed like an oasis, and you happily devoured the Swedish superstore's most popular dish, Swedish meatballs with mashed potatoes. I grew up eating it some weekends because my parents just loved the place.

I make my Swedish meatballs with a combination of pork and beef, then sink them into a cream gravy. The key to tender meatballs is not overworking the meat—just combine the ingredients gently but thoroughly until mixed, and then roll into balls.

Lingonberry sauce is the traditional accompaniment, but given that lingonberries are in short supply here in Northern California, I make a tangy fruit jam with blackberries instead. Serve mashed potatoes or buttered egg noodles alongside to soak up that gravy.

MAKE THE JAM: In a small saucepan, combine the blackberries, brown sugar, lemon juice, vanilla, and salt. Bring to a simmer over medium heat and cook until the berries have begun to soften and break down, about 5 minutes. Gently mash with a wooden spoon and continue to simmer until the jam has thickened, about 10 minutes. Remove from heat and cover until you're ready to serve.

FORM AND COOK THE MEATBALLS: In a large bowl, combine the pork, beef, panko, shallots, garlic, egg, salt, and pepper. Using a small cookie scoop or spoon, form the mixture into meatballs about 1 inch in diameter and transfer to a large plate.

Heat the olive oil in a large skillet over medium-high heat. Add the meatballs and sear, turning occasionally, until browned on all sides, about 6 minutes. Transfer to a clean plate and set aside. Wipe out the pan with a paper towel.

GRAVY

2 tablespoons unsalted butter

2 tablespoons all-purpose flour

2 cups beef stock

½ cup heavy cream

1 tablespoon light soy sauce

1 teaspoon Dijon mustard

⅛ teaspoon freshly ground black pepper

Kosher salt, to taste

Chopped dill, for garnish (optional)

MAKE THE GRAVY: Add the butter to the same pan and heat over medium-high heat until melted. Whisk in the flour and cook until lightly browned, about 30 seconds. Whisk in the stock and cream and bring to a boil. Add the soy sauce, mustard, and pepper. Let cook until reduced slightly, 3 to 4 minutes. Return the meatballs to the pan, reduce the heat to medium, and cook, covered, until the meatballs register 165°F, about 5 minutes. Season the gravy to taste with salt.

Serve the meatballs with gravy spooned over the top and the blackberry jam on the side. For a complete meal, serve over mashed potatoes or egg noodles and garnish with dill, if using.

HONEY-GARLIC
LAMB CHOPS

SERVES
4

MARINADE AND LAMB CHOPS

1 cup coconut aminos (or light soy sauce)

1 tablespoon sambal oelek

8 garlic cloves, peeled and crushed

3 green onions, chopped

1 tablespoon kosher salt

1 teaspoon freshly ground black pepper

8 bone-in lamb loin chops (3 to 4 ounces each)

1 tablespoon extra-virgin olive oil

HONEY GLAZE

¼ cup honey

1 tablespoon grated lemon zest

1 tablespoon fresh lemon juice

2 teaspoons sambal oelek (optional)

½ teaspoon freshly ground black pepper

3 tablespoons finely chopped fresh chives

These finger-licking chops are marinated in coconut aminos, sambal, and lots of garlic, quickly pan-fried, and then finished in the oven. The marinade makes them incredibly flavorful, but it's the roasted chops' final toss in a sweet-spicy honey glaze that really takes them over the top. Serve with rice and your favorite green vegetable.

MARINATE AND COOK THE CHOPS: In a plastic zip-top bag, combine the coconut aminos, sambal, garlic, green onions, salt, and pepper. Add the lamb chops, seal the bag, and shake gently to distribute the marinade over the meat. Let marinate at room temperature for 2 hours (just 1 hour if you live in a hot climate) or overnight in the refrigerator.

Preheat the oven to 400°F and set a rimmed baking sheet nearby. Heat a large, heavy skillet over high heat. Add the olive oil and, as soon as the oil is shimmering, add half the lamb chops. Sear the chops to a deep golden brown, 2 to 3 minutes per side, then transfer to the baking sheet. Repeat with the remaining chops.

Transfer the baking sheet to the oven and roast the chops until an instant-read thermometer inserted into the thickest part registers 125°F for medium rare, about 9 minutes.

MEANWHILE, MAKE THE GLAZE: In a large bowl, stir together the honey, lemon zest and juice, sambal (if using), pepper, and chives.

Remove the chops from the oven and let rest for 5 minutes. Transfer to the bowl with the honey glaze and toss to coat. Transfer to a serving platter and serve immediately.

LAMB MEATBALLS
with Yogurt-Dill Sauce

LAMB MEATBALLS

1 pound ground lamb

½ cup Italian seasoned bread crumbs

2 tablespoons balsamic vinegar

1 large egg

1 garlic clove, minced

1 teaspoon sweet paprika

1 teaspoon ground cumin

¼ teaspoon ground cinnamon

1 teaspoon kosher salt

1 teaspoon freshly ground black pepper

2 tablespoons extra-virgin olive oil

YOGURT-DILL SAUCE

1 cup plain Greek yogurt

2 tablespoons chopped fresh dill

Grated zest and juice of ½ lemon

Kosher salt and freshly ground black pepper, to taste

My kids love meatballs of all kinds, and these, flavored with cumin and cinnamon, are no exception. You can serve them for a family supper with rice or orzo alongside, or make them a bit smaller and serve them as hors d'oeuvres. If you can't find ground lamb (or aren't a fan), make them with ground beef instead.

This is a great meal to prepare with the kids because they can get their hands messy and help roll the meat mixture into balls. It's also great to double or quadruple the recipe and make enough to freeze for lazy rainy days!

MAKE THE MEATBALLS: Preheat the oven to 350°F. In a large bowl, combine the lamb, bread crumbs, vinegar, egg, garlic, paprika, cumin, cinnamon, salt, and pepper and mix gently but thoroughly until combined—don't overmix, or the meatballs will be tough. Roll the mixture into 1½-inch balls and set on a rimmed baking sheet.

Heat the olive oil in a large skillet over medium-high heat. Add the meatballs and cook, turning once, until browned on all sides, 3 to 4 minutes total. Return to the baking sheet. Transfer to the oven and bake for 10 to 15 minutes, until cooked through and browned.

WHILE THE MEATBALLS BAKE, MAKE THE SAUCE: In a small bowl, stir together the yogurt, dill, lemon zest, and lemon juice. Season to taste with salt and pepper.

Transfer the meatballs to a serving platter and serve with the yogurt-dill sauce alongside.

PORK CHOPS

with Asparagus & Mushrooms

SERVES
4

2 tablespoons Dijon mustard

2 tablespoons unsalted butter, softened

2 teaspoons honey

1 teaspoon fresh lemon juice

2 teaspoons fresh thyme leaves, minced

2 garlic cloves, minced

1 small shallot, minced

½ teaspoon kosher salt, plus more to taste

¼ teaspoon freshly ground black pepper, plus more to taste

1 bunch fat asparagus spears, woody ends trimmed

8 ounces cremini mushrooms, stemmed and sliced

1 tablespoon extra-virgin olive oil

4 boneless pork loin chops (½ inch thick and 5 to 6 ounces each)

This meal always gives me a French bistro feeling—the combination of pork, mustard, and mushrooms feels like something you'd have at a cozy Paris neighborhood joint. For this recipe, choose fatter spears of asparagus—the pencil-thin ones will overcook before the pork is done.

Preheat the oven to 400°F. In a small bowl, stir together the mustard, butter, honey, lemon juice, thyme, garlic, shallot, salt, and pepper.

Arrange the asparagus in a single layer on one-third of a rimmed baking sheet. Place the mushrooms next to the asparagus in another third of the sheet. Drizzle all with the olive oil. Place the pork chops on the remaining third of the baking sheet and season everything with salt and pepper. Slather half of the Dijon mixture on top of the chops.

Bake for 10 minutes, then turn the pork chops over and spread the remaining Dijon mixture on the other side. Continue baking until the asparagus and mushrooms are tender, and an instant-read thermometer inserted in the thickest part of the pork chop registers 145°F, about 10 minutes more. Transfer the vegetables and pork to a serving platter and let rest for 5 minutes before serving.

SHEET PAN SAUSAGE
with Peppers & Onions

SERVES
4

1 red bell pepper, cored, seeded, and sliced

1 orange bell pepper, cored, seeded, and sliced

1 medium sweet onion, sliced

1 tablespoon extra-virgin olive oil

½ teaspoon kosher salt, plus more to taste

¼ teaspoon freshly ground black pepper, plus more to taste

4 sweet or hot Italian sausage links, or a combination

This is a simple way to make ballpark-quality sausages without turning on the grill (or heading to the stadium). You can use any color of bell pepper you like (or a mix), and your favorite type of sausage (as long as it's not a pre-cooked variety). I like to serve the sausages on pretzel hot dog buns with the peppers and onions piled on top and spicy brown mustard on the side. But you can skip the buns, if you'd like, and just serve a salad alongside.

Preheat the oven to 400°F and line a rimmed baking sheet with parchment paper.

In a large bowl, combine the peppers and onion. Drizzle with the olive oil and sprinkle with salt and pepper. Toss to coat, then spread out on the prepared baking sheet and lay the sausages on top. Bake until the sausages are cooked through and the vegetables are tender, about 30 minutes.

Season the vegetables with additional salt and pepper to taste and serve with the sausages (and buns and mustard, if you like).

FOR GOOD MEASURE

SALADS & VEGGIE SIDES

ARUGULA, CHERRY TOMATO & MOZZARELLA SALAD

with Balsamic Dressing

SERVES

4

3 tablespoons extra-virgin olive oil

2 tablespoons balsamic vinegar

1 teaspoon finely chopped fresh shallot

1 garlic clove, minced

½ teaspoon brown sugar

¼ teaspoon kosher salt, plus more to taste

Generous pinch freshly ground black pepper, plus more to taste

8 ounces baby arugula

1 cup cherry tomatoes, halved

8 ounces fresh mozzarella pearls

Arugula is my go-to green when I want to make a hearty salad for my family and me. Its peppery flavor melds well with the sweetness from the brown sugar–balsamic dressing. And I love that all you really need is a bowl and a lidded jar to create this whole meal. You can eat it on its own, or add a protein of your choice. And if you don't like arugula as much as I do, you can substitute any leafy green.

Combine the olive oil, vinegar, shallot, garlic, brown sugar, salt, and pepper in a lidded jar, cap the jar, and shake vigorously to mix. (Alternatively, whisk the ingredients together in a medium bowl.)

Put the arugula in a medium salad bowl and top with the tomatoes and mozzarella. Drizzle with the dressing and toss gently to combine. Season with additional salt and pepper to taste. Serve right away.

GRAPEFRUIT, GOAT CHEESE & PINE NUT SALAD

SERVES

4

1 Ruby Red grapefruit

DRESSING

¼ cup extra-virgin olive oil

1½ tablespoons apple cider vinegar

1½ teaspoons honey

Kosher salt and freshly ground black pepper, to taste

SALAD

4 cups packed mixed greens

1 cup shredded Brussels sprouts

1 English cucumber, peeled and thinly sliced into half-moons

3 ounces goat cheese (chèvre), crumbled

¼ cup pine nuts or sunflower seeds, lightly toasted

Make this citrusy salad in the colder months when the produce section of the grocery store is looking a little sad without the abundant variety of August. Shredded Brussels sprouts stand in for some of the greens, and goat cheese and pine nuts provide a lush counterpoint to the citrus. If you prefer, you can substitute two navel or Cara Cara oranges in place of the grapefruit, or use 3 or 4 tangerines.

Using a sharp knife, cut the peel and white pith from the grapefruit; discard. Working over a small bowl, cut between the membranes to release the grapefruit segments into the bowl. Squeeze the juice from membranes into a lidded jar; add any accumulated juices from the bowl with the segments.

MAKE THE DRESSING: To the jar with the grapefruit juice, add the olive oil, vinegar, honey, and generous pinches of salt and pepper. Cap the jar and shake vigorously. (Alternatively, whisk the ingredients together in a medium bowl.)

ASSEMBLE THE SALAD: In a large bowl, combine the grapefruit segments with the greens, Brussels sprouts, and cucumber slices. Drizzle with the dressing and toss gently to combine, then top with goat cheese and nuts. Serve right away.

AVOCADO-CUCUMBER SALAD

SERVES

4

2 large Hass avocados, pitted, peeled, and cubed

1 English cucumber, diced

1 small shallot, minced

¼ cup roughly chopped fresh cilantro leaves

3 tablespoons extra-virgin olive oil

1½ tablespoons lemon juice

½ teaspoon brown sugar

¾ teaspoon kosher salt, plus more to taste

¼ teaspoon freshly ground black pepper, plus more to taste

Like guacamole, this recipe depends on the quality of your avocados to be successful. A ripe avocado should yield to firm, gentle pressure. If it's rock hard, it's not ripe; if it's very soft, it's too far gone. I love the salad with the Sheet Pan Shrimp Fajitas (page 118) or Pressure-Cooker Pulled Pork Tacos (page 144). It's creamy, crunchy, and cool—and dead simple to throw together.

In a medium salad bowl, combine the avocado, cucumber, shallot, and cilantro. In a small bowl, whisk together the olive oil, lemon juice, brown sugar, salt, and pepper. Pour over the salad and toss gently to combine; season with additional salt and pepper. Serve right away.

MEXICAN-STYLE
GRILLED CORN SALAD

SERVES

4

6 ears corn, shucked

2 tablespoons canola oil

½ cup crumbled cotija cheese

1 small red onion, finely diced

½ cup chopped fresh cilantro leaves

1 jalapeño chile, stemmed, seeded, and finely chopped

¼ cup mayonnaise

1 teaspoon smoked paprika

½ teaspoon ground cumin

¼ teaspoon kosher salt

¼ teaspoon freshly ground black pepper

1 lime, cut into wedges

Hot sauce, such as Tapatío, to taste (optional)

This salad is inspired by elote, the Mexican street food snack of corn-on-the-cob slathered in mayonnaise, rolled in cheese, and doused in hot sauce. I like to grill the corn for my salad, which gives it a slight char and a little more texture, but you can also make the salad with boiled corn; the smoked paprika still gives the salad some nice smoky flavor. If you can't find cotija cheese, substitute crumbled queso fresca or feta.

Lovers of traditional elote: Please note that this is definitely *inspired by* the original. That's one of the reasons I love cooking: You can be as interpretive as you like at any given moment.

Heat a gas or charcoal grill for direct, medium-high heat grilling. (Alternatively, set a grill pan over medium-high heat.)

Rub the corn with the oil. When the grill is hot, add the corn and grill on all sides until charred and slightly cooked, 8 to 10 minutes. Remove from heat and let cool slightly.

Cut the corn kernels from the cob into a large bowl. Add the cotija, onion, cilantro, and jalapeño and stir to mix. In a small bowl, whisk together the mayonnaise, smoked paprika, cumin, salt, and pepper. Add to the corn and mix to coat. The salad can be served right away but will keep, refrigerated, for up to a day. Serve with lime wedges and hot sauce.

BEET, WALNUT & GOAT CHEESE SALAD

with Maple Dressing

¼ cup extra-virgin olive oil

3 tablespoons maple syrup

2 tablespoons balsamic vinegar

1 tablespoon lemon juice

1 teaspoon Dijon mustard

¾ teaspoon kosher salt

¼ teaspoon freshly ground black pepper

4 medium red beets, cooked and peeled (see Note), then cubed

5 ounces arugula

4 ounces fresh goat cheese (chèvre), crumbled

½ cup walnuts, lightly toasted and roughly chopped

½ cup golden raisins

I like beets in many forms: I make a beet-ginger juice for a zippy morning pick-me-up and a beet and orange soup on cold days, but most often I serve them tossed in this simple salad, where their earthiness is tempered by a maple-balsamic dressing, toasted walnuts, and creamy goat cheese. You can use red beets, golden beets, or the beautiful striped Chioggia beets for this recipe. Many stores now sell precooked beets, which makes the salad a snap to prepare; but if you're starting with the raw beets, I've given instructions for cooking them in the Note below.

In a lidded jar, combine the olive oil, maple syrup, vinegar, lemon juice, mustard, salt, and pepper. Cap the jar and shake vigorously to combine. (Alternatively, whisk the ingredients together in a medium bowl.)

Put the beets in a small bowl, add half of the dressing, and toss to coat.

Place the arugula in a large salad bowl, add the remaining dressing, and toss gently to coat. Top with the beets, followed by the goat cheese, walnuts, and raisins. Serve immediately.

Note

You can purchase precooked beets in the refrigerated section of many grocery stores, including Trader Joe's and Costco. But if you'd like to cook beets at home, try one of these two methods:

ROAST: Preheat the oven to 400°F. Place washed but unpeeled medium beets on a large square of aluminum foil and drizzle with a few teaspoons of extra-virgin olive oil. Wrap tightly in the foil and place the packet on a baking sheet. Roast until a small paring knife inserted to the center of each beet pierces them very easily. Depending on their size, this will take 50 to 60 minutes. Unwrap the beets and set aside for 10 to 15 minutes, until cool enough to handle. Peel the beets with a small, sharp knife right over the piece of foil to prevent staining your cutting board. Use rubber gloves if you want to avoid staining your hands.

STEAM: Peel beets and slice into ½- or ¾-inch-thick slices. Bring 1 inch water to boil in a medium or large saucepan. Place a steamer insert or basket into pan and add the sliced beets. Reduce the heat so the water is vigorously simmering, cover the pot, and steam the beets until easily pierced with the tip of a paring knife, about 15 minutes. Let cool, then dice.

HEIRLOOM TOMATO, CUCUMBER & RED ONION SALAD

SERVES
4 to 6

1 pound heirloom tomatoes, cored and diced

1 thin-skinned English cucumber or 2 Persian cucumbers, halved lengthwise and sliced into half-moons

½ small red onion, thinly sliced

¼ cup fresh basil leaves, roughly chopped

2 tablespoons extra-virgin olive oil

1 tablespoon red wine vinegar

1½ teaspoons light brown sugar

Kosher salt and freshly ground black pepper, to taste

This simple salad is on repeat at our place once good tomatoes are in season. For the prettiest salad, use many different colors of tomatoes—and throw in some halved cherry tomatoes if you've got them. You can make the dressing ahead, but this salad is best eaten shortly after it's assembled. (And please, don't refrigerate it—refrigerator-cold tomatoes are not your friend!)

As the salad sits, juices will accumulate in the bowl; use some crusty bread to mop them up.

In a large bowl, combine the tomatoes, cucumber, onion, and basil.

In a lidded jar, combine the olive oil, vinegar, and sugar. Cap the jar and shake vigorously to combine. (Alternatively, whisk the ingredients together in a medium bowl.) Season to taste with salt and pepper.

Pour the dressing over the salad and toss gently to combine, then season to taste with additional salt and pepper. If you have time, let stand for 20 to 30 minutes before serving to allow the flavors to develop and all those delicious tomato juices to accumulate in the bowl.

GRILLED ROMAINE

with "Almost Caesar" Dressing

½ cup mayonnaise

2 tablespoons fresh lemon juice

1 tablespoon Worcestershire sauce

½ teaspoon Dijon mustard

1 garlic clove, minced

½ cup grated Parmigiano-Reggiano, plus more for serving

Kosher salt and freshly ground black pepper, to taste

Two romaine hearts

Extra-virgin olive oil, for brushing

Croutons, for serving

Caesar salad is definitely a household favorite. My husband tends to order it whenever he sees it on a restaurant menu, and it pairs perfectly with so many meals, from steak to pasta. My version has a few subtle tweaks that take it to another level: By grilling the romaine, you get a slightly charred, wilted, and smoky dish. And the Caesar-like dressing is perfect for even the most squeamish, since it doesn't have any actual anchovies in it. (The tanginess of the Worcestershire gives you that needed punch because anchovies are one of its main ingredients. Who would have known?)

In a medium bowl, whisk together the mayonnaise, lemon juice, Worcestershire sauce, mustard, garlic, and Parmigiano until combined. Season to taste with salt and pepper. The dressing can be made a day ahead; store in a lidded jar in the refrigerator and let stand at room temperature for 30 minutes before using.

Preheat a gas or charcoal grill for direct, medium-high heat grilling. (Alternatively, preheat a grill pan over medium-high heat.) Cut each romaine heart in half lengthwise and brush the cut side of each half lightly with olive oil. Place the romaine hearts on the grill cut-side down (if you're using a grill pan, you'll likely have to do this in batches) and grill until lightly charred, 3 to 4 minutes. Transfer the grilled romaine hearts to a platter, cut-side up, and drizzle generously with the dressing. Top with additional Parmigiano, black pepper, and croutons. Serve right away.

MY GO-TO
QUINOA SALAD

SERVES 4

DRESSING

¼ cup extra-virgin olive oil

Juice of 1 lime

2 tablespoons plain Greek yogurt

1 tablespoon balsamic vinegar

1 tablespoon honey

1 teaspoon Dijon mustard

1 teaspoon light soy sauce

Kosher salt and freshly ground black pepper, to taste

SALAD

3 cups cooked quinoa

1 Hass avocado, pitted, peeled, and cubed

½ cup crumbled feta cheese

½ cup finely diced red bell pepper

1 cup cherry tomatoes, halved (or quartered if large)

¼ cup finely diced red onion

¼ cup finely chopped fresh cilantro leaves

I spend a lot of time on planes and in cars. It's nice to pack something healthy to eat on the go, so I often turn to this salad. It's hearty enough to fuel me up for whatever's on the agenda, but it doesn't get sad if it sits at room temperature for a while. You can use other vegetables in here, too—diced cucumbers are great, or sugar snap peas, or you could add some rinsed canned beans to make it even more robust. It's also great topped with some room-temperature Seared Spiced Salmon (page 95) if you want a heartier lunch.

MAKE THE DRESSING: In a lidded jar, combine the olive oil, lime juice, yogurt, vinegar, honey, mustard, soy sauce, and salt and pepper to taste. Cap the jar and shake vigorously to combine. (Alternatively, whisk the ingredients together in a medium bowl.)

ASSEMBLE THE SALAD: In a large bowl, combine the quinoa, avocado, feta, bell pepper, tomatoes, onion, and cilantro. Pour half the dressing over and toss gently to combine; add additional dressing to taste (extra dressing will keep, refrigerated, for 3 days). Season to taste with additional salt and pepper.

EDAMAME SALAD

with Lemon-Maple Vinaigrette

SERVES

6 to 8

1 shallot, minced

1 garlic clove, minced

¼ cup extra-virgin olive oil

Juice of 1 Meyer lemon

2 tablespoons white wine vinegar

2 tablespoons maple syrup

Kosher salt, to taste

4 cups mesclun greens or spring mix (about 5 ounces)

2 large carrots, peeled and shaved into ribbons with a vegetable peeler

2 cups shelled edamame (thawed if frozen)

My kids love edamame, and I love to watch them gobble them down because the bright green soybeans are high in protein. They don't last long on our countertops because of this, so be sure to purchase extra at the store. I love this salad because it's a bit more exciting than just serving steamed edamame in their pods with salt.

If you buy your edamame fresh and still in the shell, have your kiddos shell them! Mine love this job.

In a lidded jar, combine the shallot, garlic, olive oil, lemon juice, vinegar, maple syrup, and a few generous pinches of salt. Cover and shake well to combine; season to taste with additional salt. (Alternatively, whisk the ingredients together in a medium bowl.)

In a medium salad bowl, combine the mesclun, carrot ribbons, and edamame. Drizzle the dressing over and toss gently to coat. Serve right away.

BROWN BUTTER–APPLE
SWEET POTATO MASH

3 pounds Hannah sweet potatoes, peeled and cut into 1-inch cubes

Kosher salt

2 tablespoons unsalted butter

1 small shallot, finely diced

2 garlic cloves, minced

1 sweet-tart apple, such as Golden Delicious, peeled, cored, and finely diced

¼ cup mayonnaise

½ cup half-and-half

Freshly ground black pepper, to taste

Finely sliced green onion or chives, for garnish

For this recipe I like to use Hannah sweet potatoes. They're slightly sweet (but less so than the orange-fleshed Garnet yams you'd traditionally use for candied yams), with pale yellow flesh and a starchy texture similar to that of a white potato. They make a good mash, especially one enhanced by apples cooked in nutty brown butter. This would be a great addition to your Thanksgiving feast, but I *love* to serve it with the Poached Halibut with Champagne Beurre Blanc on page 88. It's the perfect pairing.

Put the sweet potatoes in a large saucepan and add water to cover. Generously salt the water. Bring to a boil over high heat and boil until the potatoes are tender, about 15 minutes. Drain, then pass through a ricer back into the saucepan (or return to the saucepan and mash with a potato masher).

While the potatoes cook, melt the butter in a medium skillet over medium heat. The butter will foam, then begin to turn golden and smell nutty. At that point, add the shallot and cook, stirring, until translucent but not browned, about 3 minutes. Add the garlic and cook 1 minute more, then stir in the apple and continue cooking, stirring occasionally, until the apple cubes are just tender and beginning to brown, about 5 minutes.

Add the sautéed apple mixture to the pot containing the potatoes, along with the mayonnaise and half-and-half, and stir to combine. Season to taste with salt and pepper. Rewarm gently over low heat until hot, then transfer to a serving bowl and garnish with the green onions. Serve immediately.

LEMONY
ASPARAGUS

SERVES

4

1 pound asparagus, woody ends trimmed

2 tablespoons extra-virgin olive oil

½ teaspoon kosher salt, plus more to taste

Grated zest and juice of ½ Meyer lemon

There are some asparagus recipes that are best made with the skinny, pencil-like spears, but for this side dish I like the fatter ones because you can char them a bit without overcooking them. Balance the tartness of the lemon by using a generous hand with the salt.

Spread the asparagus on a plate or rimmed baking sheet. Drizzle with the olive oil and sprinkle with the salt. Heat a large cast-iron or other heavy-bottomed skillet over medium-high heat. When the pan is hot, add the asparagus and sauté, turning the spears with tongs, until tender and lightly charred in spots, about 5 minutes. Remove from the heat and add the lemon zest and juice. Transfer the asparagus to a platter, season to taste with additional salt, and serve warm or at room temperature.

COCONUT RICE

SERVES

6

2 tablespoons extra-virgin olive oil

2 tablespoons sweetened coconut flakes

2 cups jasmine rice

1⅓ cups water

1 (13.5-ounce) can full-fat coconut milk, shaken

Generous pinch kosher salt

Grated zest and juice of 1 lime

If you're looking for an alternative to plain white rice, try this coconutty variation: I add a small amount of toasted sweetened coconut flakes to uncooked jasmine rice, then replace some of the water with coconut milk. The fat can often rise to the top of a can of coconut milk, so I shake it vigorously to emulsify before opening. This rice is great with the Sweet and Spicy Scallops (page 92) or Black Pepper Steak (page 143).

Heat the olive oil in a large saucepan over medium heat. Add the coconut flakes and cook, stirring, until lightly toasted, 2 to 3 minutes. Add the rice and toast for 1 minute. Pour in the water, coconut milk, and a generous pinch of salt, stir to combine, and bring to a boil. Reduce the heat to low, cover, and cook until the rice has absorbed all the liquid, 40 minutes. Remove from the heat and let stand, covered, for 10 minutes. Uncover, fluff with a fork, and stir in the lime zest and juice. Serve right away.

CREAMY
PARSNIP PUREE

SERVES
4

8 parsnips (about 2½ pounds), peeled and chopped into 1-inch pieces

Kosher salt

1 cup heavy cream, warmed

½ cup shredded Gruyère cheese

1 tablespoon honey

2 teaspoons kosher salt

¼ teaspoon ground white pepper

1 serrano chile, halved and seeded (optional)

Chopped fresh flat-leaf parsley, for garnish

Parsnips—which resemble and are related to carrots—are a delicious alternative to potatoes. The roots become sweeter after the first frost, so look for them in the winter and early spring. Because they have less starch than potatoes, you can make this puree in the blender without worrying about it becoming gluey. I like to add a fresh chile, which counterbalances the sweetness, but you can omit it if you'd like. This is great with the Lamb Loin with Cherry-Balsamic Glaze on page 140.

Put the parsnips in a large saucepan and add water to cover. Bring to a boil, then generously salt the water. Boil until the parsnips are tender, about 15 minutes. Drain and transfer to a blender. Add the cream, Gruyère, honey, salt, pepper, and serrano, if using, and blend until smooth and thick. Transfer to a serving bowl and garnish with parsley.

SAUTÉED CABBAGE

SERVES

4 to 6

2 tablespoons unsalted butter

1 tablespoon minced garlic

1 small head red or green cabbage (about 1½ pounds), cored and thinly sliced

1 teaspoon kosher salt, plus more to taste

½ teaspoon whole cumin seeds

¼ teaspoon freshly ground black pepper, plus more to taste

Grated zest and juice of ½ lemon

Cabbage typically shows up in coleslaw form, but it's absolutely delicious when cut into ribbons and sautéed in butter until sweet and silky. Some garlic and cumin seeds punch up its mellow flavor.

In a large skillet over medium heat, melt the butter. Add the garlic and sauté for 1 minute. Add the cabbage and salt and sauté for 3 minutes. Add the cumin and pepper and cook, stirring, 1 minute more, until the cabbage is wilted. Remove from the heat and stir in the lemon zest and juice. Season to taste with additional salt and pepper and serve.

GINGER
CAULIFLOWER RICE

SERVES

4

1-inch piece peeled fresh ginger, grated (about 2 teaspoons)

3 fresh basil leaves

1 teaspoon sugar

1 teaspoon kosher salt

¼ teaspoon whole black peppercorns

2 teaspoons plus 3 tablespoons extra-virgin olive oil

1 medium shallot, finely diced

4 cups cauliflower rice, homemade (see Note) or store-bought

As I'm sure we all know by now…cauliflower rice is not actual rice, but it makes a great carb-free stand-in, especially when it's flavored with lots of ginger. You can buy riced cauliflower at many grocery stores (it's often in the freezer aisle), but it's also easy to make at home with a food processor. If you'd like to try, I've given instructions in the Note below.

In a mortar with a pestle or a small food processor, combine the ginger, basil, sugar, salt, peppercorns, and 2 teaspoons of the olive oil and pound or process into a paste.

Heat the remaining 3 tablespoons olive oil in a large skillet over medium-high heat. Add the shallot and cook, stirring, for 1 minute. Add the cauliflower rice and continue to cook, stirring, for about 3 minutes. Stir in the ginger paste and cook 1 minute more, then serve.

Note

To make cauliflower rice at home, start with 1 large head (about 2 pounds). Cut the cauliflower into quarters and remove the core from each piece. Break up the remaining cauliflower into large florets. Transfer the cauliflower to a food processor and process until reduced to couscous-size pieces (if necessary, do this in two batches). If you do not have a food processor, you can also grate the florets on the large holes of a box grater; you should end up with 4 cups of cauliflower rice.

Hoisin-Glazed
Sea Bass, page 100

SUMAC-ROASTED
CARROTS

5 large carrots, peeled and cut into 4- by ½-inch batons

2 tablespoons extra-virgin olive oil

1 teaspoon maple syrup or honey

2 teaspoons ground sumac

½ teaspoon kosher salt, plus more to taste

¼ teaspoon freshly ground black pepper, plus more to taste

Fresh thyme leaves, for garnish

Lemon juice, for finishing

I first learned of sumac through Michael Mina (aka my favorite chef in the whole wide world—and my partner in International Smoke). It is a brick-red spice made from the ground berries of the sumac bush. It has a tart, lemony flavor and is a wonderful complement to sweet roasted carrots. If you can find small bunch carrots, you can roast them whole.

Preheat the oven to 400°F. Spread the carrots in a single layer on a rimmed baking sheet and drizzle with the olive oil and maple syrup. Sprinkle the sumac, salt, and pepper over and toss to coat.

Roast until the carrots are tender and lightly browned, 18 to 20 minutes. Transfer to a platter, garnish with fresh thyme, and season with additional salt and pepper and lemon juice to taste. Serve warm or at room temperature.

JAMAICAN-STYLE
RICE & PEAS

1 tablespoon canola oil

2 green onions, finely chopped

2 teaspoons minced fresh ginger

3 garlic cloves, minced

1 (15-ounce) can pigeon peas (or black-eyed peas), drained and rinsed

1 cup water

1 (13.5-ounce) can coconut milk, shaken

3 fresh thyme sprigs

1 whole Scotch bonnet or habanero chile

2 cups long-grain white rice

This is a staple Jamaican recipe that I grew up eating and now make frequently for my own family. It's traditionally made with either pigeon peas or kidney beans. Every cook seasons their pot of rice and peas according to their own tastes, but when I consulted my mother and aunts for their recipes, the consensus was that it should include green onions, ginger, and garlic, with some gentle heat from the addition of a Scotch bonnet chile that you drop in whole and remove before serving. This is a great side dish alongside jerk or simply grilled chicken.

Heat the oil in a large saucepan over medium heat. Add the green onions, ginger, and garlic and cook, stirring, for about 1 minute, until fragrant. Pour in the peas and water, then stir in the coconut milk. Drop in the thyme and the whole chile. Bring to a boil, then reduce to a gentle simmer and simmer for 10 minutes, stirring occasionally.

Stir in the rice and return to a boil. Reduce the heat to low, cover the pot, and cook for about 30 minutes, until the rice is tender and the liquid is absorbed. Remove from the heat and let stand, covered, for 10 minutes. Uncover, remove and discard the chile and thyme sprigs, and fluff the rice with a fork. Serve.

WASABI
MASHED POTATOES

SERVES

4

6 medium Yukon Gold potatoes (about 2½ pounds), peeled and cut into 2-inch cubes

Kosher salt

¾ cup half-and-half or heavy cream, warmed

6 tablespoons unsalted butter, softened

¼ cup mayonnaise

1½ tablespoons wasabi paste

1 teaspoon grated lemon zest

These are mashed potatoes with a sophisticated twist. Now, wasabi may sound a little intimidating, but trust me—it's not. While fresh wasabi root (also known as Japanese horseradish) can be hard to find, wasabi paste is easy to source, and delivers the same spicy flavor.

My trick to ultra-creamy mashed potatoes is simple: Add mayonnaise! Using a bit of mayonnaise in addition to the half-and-half and butter results in silky, light mashed potatoes. This trick is especially useful if you're preparing the potatoes ahead (at Thanksgiving, for example). Butter solidifies when cold, so potatoes made only with butter will harden up and lose their silky texture when refrigerated. But mashed potatoes with a bit of mayo remain silky and soft, even after they've been refrigerated. I like to serve these mashed potatoes with the Lamb Meatballs with Yogurt-Dill Sauce (page 153).

Put the potatoes in a large saucepan and add water to cover. Generously salt the water, bring to a boil over high heat, and boil until the potatoes are fork tender, about 15 minutes. Drain and pass through a potato ricer back into the pot. (If you don't have a ricer, return the potatoes to the pot and mash with a hand masher.) Add the half-and-half, butter, mayonnaise, wasabi paste, and lemon zest and mix to combine. Season to taste with additional salt. Serve hot.

ROASTED
PURPLE SWEET POTATOES
with Romesco Sauce

2 pounds medium purple sweet potatoes

Kosher salt

ROMESCO SAUCE

1 (12-ounce) jar roasted red peppers, drained

½ cup lightly toasted blanched almonds or cashews

Juice of ½ lemon

1 garlic clove, peeled

1 teaspoon kosher salt, plus more to taste

½ teaspoon sugar

¼ teaspoon sambal oelek or chili paste

¼ cup extra-virgin olive oil

I love the combination of roasted sweet potatoes and romesco, a thick Spanish sauce made from roasted red peppers and nuts. The potatoes are sweet, and the sauce is tangy, salty, and a little spicy. Purple sweet potatoes, which have vibrant violet flesh (and are also high in vitamin C), are especially beautiful alongside the romesco, but if you can't find them, substitute orange-fleshed Garnet, Beauregard, or Jewel sweet potatoes. These sweet potatoes are baked in their jackets, but you could also slice them into wedges and toss them with a bit of oil before roasting for 30 to 40 minutes, if you're looking for something with a crispy-crunchy edge.

Preheat the oven to 425°F and line a baking sheet with aluminum foil.

Rinse the potatoes, place on the prepared baking sheet, and sprinkle generously with salt. Use a paring knife to poke a few holes into each potato. Roast until the tip of a paring knife slips easily into the potato, about 45 minutes.

WHILE THE POTATOES BAKE, MAKE THE ROMESCO: Combine the peppers, almonds, lemon juice, garlic, salt, sugar, and sambal in the bowl of a food processor and process to a chunky puree. With the motor running, drizzle in the olive oil and continue to process until the sauce is thick and smooth. Transfer to a bowl and season to taste with additional salt.

Split the potatoes and spoon some of the romesco sauce onto each.

CHAPTER

8

SWEET ENDINGS

DESSERTS

———

MAKES
10
crepes

EASY
CHOCOLATE & MANGO CREPES

3 very ripe mangoes, pitted, peeled, and coarsely chopped

1 tablespoon fresh lime juice, plus more to taste

1 tablespoon honey, plus more to taste

1 (5-ounce) package store-bought crepes (10 crepes)

½ cup Nutella

¼ cup lightly toasted chopped hazelnuts

powdered sugar, for garnish (optional)

A crepe is like a really thin pancake, and my mom made them for us a lot when I was a kid. I remember sitting on a stool and watching her whip them up in no time (without a recipe) at breakfast and sometimes for dessert. The toppings were always different. And the joy we got watching her make them was priceless.

Here, I combine Nutella and mango, which tastes out of this world. But you can do so much with a crepe, so mix and match your fillings. In this recipe, we use store-bought crepes to save time. Such a winner!

In a blender or food processor, combine the mangoes, lime juice, and honey and process until smooth, adding a few tablespoons of water as needed to aid the blending. Transfer the sauce to a bowl and season to taste with additional lime juice or honey.

Heat a medium nonstick skillet over medium-low heat. Add one crepe to the pan and heat, turning once, until warm, about 20 seconds per side. Transfer to a plate and cover with a tea towel; repeat with the remaining crepes, stacking them as you go.

Spread 1 scant tablespoon Nutella down the center of each crepe and roll into a cigar. Arrange two filled crepes on each plate, drizzle with mango sauce, and sprinkle with hazelnuts and powdered sugar (if using). Serve.

CREAMY
BUTTERSCOTCH POT FOR ONE

MAKES
1
pot de crème

½ cup butterscotch chips

1 tablespoon dark brown sugar

⅓ cup heavy cream

There is something about a butterscotch pudding that just makes you feel like a kid again. I can still see myself as a girl, ripping the lid off the top of one of those butterscotch pudding cups and savoring every bite of that delicious caramelly treat. And with half my household not loving chocolate, sometimes I have to think outside of the box when it comes to the occasional dessert. So this is my take on a pot de crème, butterscotch style!

I love how this takes very little time and effort to put together. With just three simple ingredients and a blender, you get a rich and decadent dessert. This makes one pot de crème, but you can double, triple, or quadruple the recipe as needed.

In a blender or food processor, combine the butterscotch chips and sugar and pulse until fine.

In a small pot, heat the cream until bubbles appear around the edge of the pot. Slowly pour the cream into the blender or food processor and blend or process until smooth. Pour the mixture into a small jar or bowl and refrigerate until cooled and set, 1 hour. Serve with whipped cream on top, if desired.

STONE FRUIT
BREAD PUDDING

BREAD PUDDING

1½ cups heavy cream

1 cup whole milk

4 large eggs

½ cup packed light brown sugar

2 tablespoons bourbon (optional)

1 teaspoon vanilla extract, homemade (page 220) or store-bought

1 teaspoon ground cinnamon

1 teaspoon ground nutmeg

¼ teaspoon ground cloves

Pinch of kosher salt

3 tablespoons unsalted butter

2½ cups diced fresh peaches or nectarines (or other stone fruit of your choice)

1 loaf day-old brioche (or challah) bread, cut into 1-inch cubes (7 to 8 cups)

CARAMEL SAUCE

½ cup (1 stick) unsalted butter

1 cup packed light brown sugar

¼ teaspoon ground cinnamon

¼ teaspoon ground nutmeg

¼ teaspoon kosher salt

¼ cup heavy cream

Toasted pecans and whipped cream, for garnish (optional)

Lord knows, I *love* bread pudding. The whole family does, really. It's overly—yet perfectly—indulgent and allows a sense of escape from the realities of carbs. When a bread pudding is set in front of you, the word *carbohydrate* should not and cannot exist.

I like to deem myself the "bread pudding princess" of my family, but only because my mom must reign queen. I am so passionate about bread puddings that they are the cafe feature at my Sweet July store in Oakland. If you're ever in the area, come give it a try! If not, *make this.*

I bake a version of this bread pudding all summer long, using day-old brioche or challah and whatever stone fruit is ripest and juiciest, beginning with apricots, then switching to peaches, plums, and nectarines as the season progresses. The caramel sauce really just puts this over the top to please even the bougiest of guests. Ha!

Preheat the oven to 350°F.

MAKE THE BREAD PUDDING: In a large bowl, whisk together the cream, milk, eggs, brown sugar, bourbon (if using), vanilla, cinnamon, nutmeg, cloves, and salt.

Melt the butter in a 12-inch cast-iron skillet over medium heat. When the butter stops foaming and begins to brown, slowly pour it into the custard mixture, then stir in the peaches. Arrange the cubed bread in the now-empty skillet and pour the custard mixture over. Bake for 45 to 55 minutes, until the liquid is absorbed and the top is golden brown.

WHEN THE BREAD PUDDING HAS ABOUT 15 MINUTES REMAINING TO BAKE, MAKE THE SAUCE: In a saucepan, combine the butter, brown sugar, cinnamon, nutmeg, and salt over medium heat. Once the butter and sugar have melted and the mixture is smooth, pour in the cream and whisk until smooth. Remove from the heat.

Serve the bread pudding with the warm sauce generously spooned over the top. Garnish with toasted pecans and whipped cream (if desired).

ALMOND BUTTER COOKIES

MAKES

2 dozen

cookies

1 cup creamy almond butter, at room temperature

½ cup packed dark brown sugar

1 large egg

½ teaspoon vanilla extract, homemade (page 220) or store-bought

⅛ teaspoon kosher salt

I love a good sweet nutty treat! (Save your laughs, people.) These cookies are the perfect bite-size dessert or midday pick-me-up, and they're made with ingredients you probably already have on hand. And no, there's no mistake in the ingredient list—these cookies do not contain flour, so they're gluten-free! If you prefer, you can make the simple cookies with creamy peanut butter in place of almond butter.

Preheat the oven to 350°F and line a baking sheet with parchment paper or a silicone baking mat.

In a large mixing bowl, stir together the almond butter, sugar, egg, vanilla, and salt until combined and smooth.

With a small scoop or spoon, scoop out tablespoons of dough onto the prepared baking sheet, spacing them about 2 inches apart. With the tines of a fork, press down lightly on the tops of each cookie to form a crosshatch pattern. Bake until golden brown, 8 to 10 minutes. Let cool for 5 minutes on the baking sheet, then transfer to a wire rack to cool completely. These are best eaten the same day they're baked, though they'll keep in a lidded container for a few days.

WHITE CHOCOLATE, CHERRY & MACADAMIA
SKILLET COOKIE

1 cup (2 sticks) unsalted butter

1½ cups packed light brown sugar

1 teaspoon vanilla extract, homemade (page 220) or store-bought

2¼ cups all-purpose flour

1 teaspoon baking soda

½ teaspoon kosher salt

2 large eggs

1 cup white chocolate chips

½ cup dried cherries, chopped

½ cup macadamia nuts, chopped

Powdered sugar, for garnish (optional)

The only thing better than a batch of cookies is one massive skillet cookie. This one, loaded with white chocolate, dried cherries, and macadamia nuts, is a favorite, though you could use bittersweet chocolate chips and a different type of nut if you prefer. The most challenging part of this recipe is waiting: The cookie should be fully cooled before you cut it into fat wedges.

Preheat the oven to 350°F.

Heat a 12-inch cast-iron skillet over medium-high heat. Add the butter and cook until melted and beginning to brown and bubble. Remove from the heat and stir in the sugar and vanilla until well combined. Let cool completely, 10 to 15 minutes.

In a medium bowl, whisk together the flour, baking soda, and salt.

One at a time, stir the eggs into the butter and sugar in the pan, followed by the flour mixture. Mix until homogeneous, then fold in the white chocolate chips, cherries, and macadamia nuts.

Smooth the mixture into an even layer in the skillet. Bake until the edges are golden brown and firm (the center will still be a bit gooey), 30 to 35 minutes. Let cool in the pan at least 1 hour, then cut into wedges and serve. Dust with powdered sugar if you're feeling fancy.

ROASTED PEARS

with Vanilla-Infused Caramel Sauce

SERVES
4

4 ripe Bosc or Bartlett pears (about 8 ounces each)

1 cup packed light brown sugar

½ cup half-and-half

4 tablespoons salted butter (or 4 tablespoons unsalted butter plus ½ teaspoon kosher salt)

2 tablespoons vanilla extract, homemade (page 220) or store-bought

Vanilla ice cream, for serving

Here's an elegant, easy, fall dessert. Roasting pears is less intense than making poached pears, and the roasting brings out all of the yummy sweet pear flavors. Use firm-ripe pears: too soft and they'll turn to mush when roasted; too firm and under-ripe and they'll remain that way even after roasting.

Wash the pears, remove the stems, and trim the bottoms so that they stand upright. Stand in a baking dish and roast for 30 to 35 minutes, until tender. When cool enough to handle, cut each pear in half and use a melon baller or 1-teaspoon measuring spoon to scoop out the seeds and core.

WHILE THE PEARS ROAST, MAKE THE SAUCE: In a medium saucepan, heat the brown sugar, half-and-half, and butter over medium heat, stirring frequently, until the mixture is smooth, coats the back of a wooden spoon, and is beginning to bubble, about 7 minutes. Remove from the heat and stir in the vanilla. Let cool slightly. The caramel sauce can be made ahead; stored in a lidded jar in the refrigerator, it will keep for a week. Reheat gently over low heat until smooth before using.

To serve, place two halves of pear on each serving plate, drizzle generously with caramel sauce, and top with a scoop of vanilla ice cream.

MAPLE-GLAZED
BACON DONUTS

Canola oil, for frying

1 tube 8-count refrigerator
biscuits

1 cup powdered sugar

¼ cup maple syrup

½ teaspoon vanilla extract,
homemade (page 220) or
store-bought

½ cup chopped cooked
bacon, for garnish

The shortcut to homemade donuts: store-bought biscuit dough! I discovered this hack a few years ago and life hasn't been the same since. The donuts are great when simply sprinkled with cinnamon sugar, but when you want to take them to the next level, the maple glaze and crumbled bacon garnish are the move.

Heat a 2-inch depth of canola oil in a Dutch oven or other large heavy-bottomed pot over medium-high heat until it registers 375°F on a deep-frying thermometer.

While the oil heats, use a 1-inch round biscuit cutter to cut the center out of each biscuit. Set a wire cooling rack over a rimmed baking sheet and set nearby. In a medium bowl, whisk together the powdered sugar, maple syrup, and vanilla until smooth.

When the oil is hot, using a slotted spoon or spider, gently lower half of the donuts and their holes into the hot oil. Fry, turning once, until golden brown on each side, 1½ to 2 minutes. Remove from the oil and transfer to the wire rack to cool. Let the oil return to temperature, then fry the remaining donuts and donut holes.

When the donuts are cool enough to handle, dip each, top-side down, into the maple glaze to coat. Return to the wire rack, and top each donut with some of the bacon. Let stand until the glaze is set, about 10 minutes, then enjoy.

RICE PUDDING

2 cups half-and-half

1½ cups cooked white rice

⅓ cup maple syrup

1 teaspoon vanilla extract, homemade (page 220) or store-bought

1 teaspoon ground cinnamon

¼ teaspoon ground ginger

⅛ teaspoon ground nutmeg

⅛ teaspoon ground cloves

Pinch kosher salt

1 large egg

¾ cup dried apricots or golden raisins

1 tablespoon unsalted butter

This version of a homey, comforting dessert is especially quick to make because it uses leftover cooked white rice, which gets briefly simmered in sweetened half-and-half seasoned with warm baking spices. Does anyone else feel like lighting a fire and putting on some cozy socks? If you don't care for raisins, substitute chopped dried apricots, figs, or prunes, or spoon some chopped fresh fruit over the top of each serving just before you dig in.

In a medium saucepan, combine 1 cup of the half-and-half, the rice, maple syrup, vanilla, cinnamon, ginger, nutmeg, cloves, and salt. Stir well to combine and bring to a boil over medium-high heat. Reduce the heat so the mixture is simmering and simmer, uncovered and stirring occasionally, until slightly reduced and thickened, 10 to 15 minutes.

In a medium bowl, whisk together the remaining 1 cup half-and-half and the egg. Whisking continuously, add a ladleful of the hot rice mixture to the milk and egg, then whisk that mixture back into the saucepan. Increase the heat slightly and cook, stirring, until the mixture thickens, 5 minutes longer. Stir in the dried fruit (apricots or raisins) and butter.

Serve warm, or let cool to room temperature, refrigerate, and serve cold.

S P I C E D
APPLE TURNOVERS
with Maple Brown Sugar Sauce

MAKES
8
turnovers

TURNOVERS

1 medium apple, peeled, cored, and diced (about 1 cup)

2 tablespoons light brown sugar

1½ teaspoons fresh lemon juice

1 teaspoon all-purpose flour

¼ teaspoon ground cinnamon

¼ teaspoon ground nutmeg

Pinch kosher salt

1 (17.3-ounce) box puff pastry, such as Pepperidge Farm, thawed but cool

Egg wash of 1 large egg beaten with 1 teaspoon water

SAUCE

¼ cup brown sugar

¼ cup maple syrup

4 tablespoons butter

1 tablespoon heavy cream

¼ teaspoon salt

½ teaspoon vanilla extract, homemade (page 220) or store-bought

Store-bought puff pastry is a gift to the busy home cook! These apple turnovers are a favorite quick fall dessert, with a maple brown sugar sauce that makes them extra special. For the crispest pastry, bake the turnovers until they're a deep golden brown—if underbaked, they'll be soggy. "And nobody likes a soggy bottom!" (That's me in my best Paul Hollywood voice.)

Preheat the oven to 425°F and line a baking sheet with parchment paper or a silicone pan liner.

In a medium bowl, combine the apple, brown sugar, lemon juice, flour, cinnamon, nutmeg, and salt and stir to mix.

Place the two thawed puff pastry sheets on a lightly floured work surface and cut each into four squares. Spoon about ¼ cup of the apple mixture on each square. Brush the edges lightly with egg wash and fold one corner over to the other corner to enclose the filling. Use a fork and press gently to seal the edges. Place the pastries on the prepared baking sheet and brush the tops with egg wash. Bake for 15 to 20 minutes, until golden brown. Transfer to a wire rack and let cool.

WHILE THE TURNOVERS BAKE, MAKE THE SAUCE: In a small saucepan over medium-low heat, whisk together the brown sugar, maple syrup, butter, heavy cream, salt, and vanilla until the sugar dissolves and the sauce is smooth and velvety.

The turnovers are best enjoyed warm with a generous helping of sauce on the side or spooned over the top.

GUAVA GINGER
ICE CREAM

1 (14-ounce) can sweetened condensed milk

½ cup guava nectar or concentrate

1 teaspoon pure vanilla extract, homemade (page 220) or store-bought

Grated zest of 1 lime

1 cup cold heavy cream

¼ cup finely chopped candied ginger

This recipe is going to blow your mind, and I am not talking about a brain freeze. There is no machine involved, no custard ice cream base, and it takes only 5 minutes to throw together—yet this ice cream is still incredibly smooth and creamy. Like, for real for real, y'all. I love the combination of guava and ginger, but you could experiment with other fruit purees, like mango or passion fruit.

In a large bowl, combine the condensed milk, guava nectar, vanilla, and lime zest.

In the bowl of an electric mixer fitted with the whisk attachment (or in a large bowl with a handheld mixer), beat the cream until it holds stiff peaks.

With a large rubber spatula, gently but thoroughly fold the whipped cream into the condensed milk mixture in two additions, taking care not to overmix. Gently fold in the candied ginger.

Pour the mixture into an 8- by 4-inch loaf pan and gently press a sheet of plastic wrap directly onto the surface of the ice cream (this prevent ice crystals from forming). Transfer to the freezer and freeze for at least 4 hours before serving. The ice cream will keep for up to 2 weeks.

HOMEMADE
VANILLA EXTRACT

MAKES ABOUT
7½
cups

1 (1.75-liter) bottle vodka

8 cardamom pods

4 (2-inch-long) cinnamon sticks

2 whole star anise

8 vanilla beans

Yes, you can buy vanilla extract, but it's very simple to make at home and keeps forever. I know that statement feels a bit Ina (who is culinary royalty), but it's seriously so easy and much more affordable! You can purchase "realllllly good"–quality Madagascar vanilla beans online (via Amazon) and make a big jar—but it does need to sit for 3 months before it's ready. Save it all for yourself, or decant it into smaller jars to give as gifts.

In a large (2-liter) lidded jar, combine the vodka, cardamom, cinnamon, star anise, and vanilla beans. Tightly seal and allow to sit for at least 3 months. No need to refrigerate; store the jar in a dry, cool place in your pantry.

As you use it, keep refilling it with vodka and vanilla bean pods.

ACKNOWLEDGMENTS

This cookbook could not have been possible without my amazing team. I like to think of them as literal angels walking the earth. I feel like it's not said enough: They do the dirty work that allows me to live out the saying "If you love what you do you never work a day in your life." So here goes it…

Team AC BRANDS: You all make my world go round. Thank you for truly understanding and leaning in to the chaos of our lives and business. Thank you also for encouraging me to "dig in" to this second cookbook and ignoring my constant nervousness. Love you all.

Eva Kolenko: You are a legend. Thank you for bringing a unique vibrancy to this book. You truly bring this all to life. It was so much fun working together. I just love everything you photograph. You're the coolest.

Maria Tarleton: My gorgeous sister! Thank you for being my partner in crime. I had so much fun spending time, cooking, and developing these recipes together!

Lillian Kang & Veronica Laramie: My beautiful food-styling team! Thank you for seeing the dishes the way I do and making them pop on the page. We always seemed to be on the same page, and it eased my nerves. (Great call on the hairless crabs ;))

Claire Mack: Thank you for making everything so gorgeous. Your aesthetic is unmatched.

Michael Szczerban: YOU ARE THE BEST EDITOR. Thank you for believing in my vision with this book, always hearing me out, and being simply the sweetest. You made this process so easy for everyone. Hope I make you proud!

My Little, Brown/Voracious Team: Thank you all so much for allowing me a go at a second cookbook. I can't believe I get to say that. You guys are incredible.

Stacey Glick: Lit agent extraordinaire. Thank you for being there since day one and always rallying for me.

Jessica Battilana: Thank you for keeping us all organized and helping me tell the story of this book.

Sandra Wu: Thank you for testing out these recipes and making sure they're smooth sailing for everyone.

Eric Lundy: Thank you for testing and being a part of this process.

Sherri McMullen: Thank you so much for making me look good!

Glam Squad! Ashley Bias & Jess Mayeux: You guys make me look and feel my best, and I can't thank you enough.

My Mama: Thank you for always inspiring me and recipe testing with me! I love you so much.

INDEX

ABOUT THE AUTHOR

Ayesha Curry is a renowned restaurateur, chef, television host, and producer, and she is the author of the *New York Times* bestselling cookbook *The Seasoned Life: Food, Family, Faith, and the Joy of Eating Well.*

Featured on the prestigious 30 Under 30 list by *Forbes* magazine, Curry takes an accessible approach to cooking and has a passion for creating easy-to-use products, which has made her one of the most sought-after experts on food and lifestyle in the world, with over nine million avid social-media followers and subscribers.

As a restaurateur, Curry teamed up with award-winning chef Michael Mina to create International Smoke, a restaurant concept featuring elevated barbecue dishes from around the globe with locations in San Francisco, San Diego, and Las Vegas.

In 2019 Curry, along with her husband, launched the family-founded charity "Eat. Learn. Play." with a mission to end childhood hunger, ensure universal access to quality education, and enable healthy, active lifestyles.

Curry lives in the Bay Area with her three children, Riley, Ryan, and Canon; her husband, Stephen; and her labradoodle, Reza-Joon.